COMFORT FOOD COOKBOOK

More of Your Classic Comfort Food Favorites

(A Collection of Classic Healthy Recipes)

Marcus Holm

Published by Alex Howard

© Marcus Holm

All Rights Reserved

Comfort Food Cookbook: More of Your Classic Comfort Food Favorites (A Collection of Classic Healthy Recipes)

ISBN 978-1-990169-28-1

All rights reserved. No part of this guide may be reproduced in any form without permission in writing from the publisher except in the case of brief quotations embodied in critical articles or reviews.

Legal & Disclaimer

The information contained in this book is not designed to replace or take the place of any form of medicine or professional medical advice. The information in this book has been provided for educational and entertainment purposes only.

The information contained in this book has been compiled from sources deemed reliable, and it is accurate to the best of the Author's knowledge; however, the Author cannot guarantee its accuracy and validity and cannot be held liable for any errors or omissions. Changes are periodically made to this book. You must consult your doctor or get professional medical advice before using any of the suggested remedies, techniques, or information in this book.

Table of contents

PART 1 1

INTRODUCTION 2

WHOLESOME HOTCAKE BREAKFAST 3

GREAT STEAK BREAKFAST 5

CRISPY CHICKEN AND WAFFLES 6

SOUTHERN STYLE AVOCADO EGG SALAD 8

GRILLED CASHEW CHEESE SANDWICH 10

WHOLLY JALAPEÑO "CORNBREAD" 12

REAL DEAL CHILI 14

EASY CHEESY FRIES 16

STACKED PORTOBELLO BURGER 18

ZESTY MEATBALL MARINARA 20

DELICIOUS EGGPLANT PARMESAN 22

ZUCCHINI PASTA LASAGNA 25

SAUTÉED SAUSAGE AND PEPPERS 27

MAC AND "CHEESE" PLEASE 28

WINTER'S NIGHT CHICKEN PIE 30

1ST PRIZE SHEPPARD'S PIE 33

SOUTHERN CHICKEN AND DUMPLINGS 36

CRUNCH-FRIED STEAK AND GRAVY 38

LIVER AND CARAMELIZED ONIONS 40

BREADED BAKED CHICKEN 42

GARLIC PARSNIP MASH 44

CHEESY CROQUETTES 45

CLASSIC BEEF PATTY 48

Ripe Banana Bread 50

Natural Pumpkin Bread 52

PART 2 54

1. RECIPE INDEX 55

1.1. Appetizers 55

1.2. Soups 55

1.3. Entrees 56

1.4. Vegetarian 57

1.5. Desserts 57

2. APPETIZERS 59

1) Bibbeliskäs (Cottage Cheese With Onions And Herbs) 59

2) Bayerische Brezen (Bavarian Pretzels) 61

3) Gebackener Camembert (Baked Camembert With Red Currant Sauce) 63

4) Obatzter (Bavarian Cheese Spread) 65

5) Markklößchensuppe (Marrow Dumplings In Double Consomme) 66

6) Badischer Wurstsalat (Bologna Salad From Baden) 69

7) Bayerischer Krautsalat (Bavarian Cabbage Salad) 70

8) Käsedip (Quick Cheesedip) 71

9) Sauerkaut-Schinken Bällchen (Kraut Ham Balls) 72

10) Rindfleisch Zwiebel Strudel (Beef Onion Strudel) 74

11) Strammer Max (Hearty German Sandwich With Egg) 76

12) Speckbrötchen (Smoked Ham Rolls) 77

13) Flammkuchen (Onion Flatbread With Bacon) 79

14) Heringssalat (Herring Salad) 82

15) Gefüllte Tomaten Mit Shrimps (Shrimp Stuffed Tomatoes) 84

3. SOUPS 85

1) GAISBURGER MARSCH (BEEF & VEGETABLE STEW WITH SPÄTZLE) 85
2) LEBERKNÖDELSUPPE (LIVER DUMPLING SOUP) 87
3) ZWIEBELSUPPE MIT DUNKLEM BIER (DARK BEER ONION SOUP) 89
4) BIER KÄSE SUPPE (CHEESE SOUP WITH GERMAN LAGER) 90
5) FLÄDLESUPPE (BROTH WITH STRIPS OF PANCAKE) 92
6) PICHELSTEINER TOPF (PICHELSTEINER STEW) 93
7) OCHSENSCHWANZSUPPE (OXTAIL SOUP) 95
8) ERDÄPFELGULASCH (CREAMY POTATO GOULASH) 97
9) GRIESSNOCKERL-SUPPE (SEMOLINA DUMPLING SOUP) 100
10) BROTSUPPE (BREAD SOUP) 102
11) BAYERISCHE PILZSUPPE (CREAM OF MUSHROOM SOUP) 104
12) KERBELSUPPE (CREAM OF CHERVIL SOUP) 106
14) SAUERKRAUT TOMATEN SUPPE (SAUERKRAUT TOMATO SOUP) 109
15) SPARGELSUPPE (WHITE ASPARAGUS SOUP) 111

4. ENTREES 113

1) RIPPCHEN MIT KRAUT (KASSELER RIPPCHEN WITH SAUERKRAUT) 113
2) RINDERROULADEN MIT KARTOFFELN UND ROTKOHL (GERMAN ROULADEN WITH POTATOES AND BRAISED RED CABBAGE) 115
3) MAULTASCHEN (SWABIAN RAVIOLIS) 118
4) ZWIEBELKUCHEN (ONION CAKE WITH BACON) 121
5) SCHWEINSHAXE IN BIER SOßE (PORK KNUCKLES IN BEER SAUCE) 123
6) BRATHENDL (OKTOBERFEST ROAST CHICKEN) 125
7) SCHWEINEBRATEN MIT KARTOFFELKLÖßEN (PORK ROAST WITH POTATO DUMPLINGS) 127
8) SCHWEINEGESCHNETZELTES (PORK STIR FRY) 129
9) ZWIEBELROSTBRATEN (PAN FRIED BEEF STEAKS WITH FRIED ONIONS) 131
10) SAUERBRATEN (GERMAN STYLE POT ROAST AND GINGERSNAP GRAVY) 132
11) FLEISCHKÜCHLE (SWABIAN MEATBALLS) 134

12) Gefüllte Gans (Roasted Duck Stuffed With Apples) 135
13) Schwarzwald Cordon Bleu (Black Forest Chicken Cordon Bleu) 138
14) Backhendl (Viennese Fried Chicken) 140
15) Wiener Schnitzel (Fried Pork Viennese) 142
5. Vegetarian 144
1) Linsen Mit Spätzle (Lentils With Spätzle) 144
2) Schupfnudeln (Finger-Thick Potato Dumplings) 146
3) Käsespätzle (Cheese Pasta) 147
4) Schwäbischer Kartoffelsalat (Swabian Potato Salad) 149
5) Zwetschgenknödel (Plum Dumplings With Cinnamon Breadcrumb Butter) 151
6) Dampfnudeln Mit Vanillesoße (German Steamed Dumplings With Vanilla Sauce) 153
7) Grünkernküchle (Green Spelt Burgers) 155
8) Kartoffelpuffer (Potato Pancakes) 157
9) Semmelknödel Mit Schwammerlsoße (Bavarian Dumplings With Mushroom Sauce) 159
10) Pellkartoffeln Mit Kräuterquark (Boiled Potatoes With Quark) 161

6. DESSERTS 162

1) Zwetschgenkuchen (Plum Cake) 162
2) Pfitzauf (Meringue Pastry) 164
3) Apfelstrudel (Apple Strudel) 165
4) Schwarzwälder Kirschcreme (Black Forest Cherry Cream Dessert) 167
5) Flambierte Crêpes Im Waldbeerenmeer (Crêpes Flambees With Forest Berry Coulis) 169
6) Rote Grütze Mit Vanillesoße (Red Berry Pudding With Vanilla Sauce) 171
7) Spaghetti Eis (Spaghetti Ice Cream) 173
8) Träubleskuchen (Swabian Redcurrant Tart) 174
9) Bienenstich (Bee Sting Cake) 176

10) Schneckennudeln (German Cinnamon Rolls) 178

11) Apfelküchle (Fried Apples) 180

12) Windbeutel (Bavarian Cream Puff) 181

13) Bayerische Creme (Bavarian Cream) 183

14) Ausgezogene (Knee Pastries) 185

15) Buchteln (Sweet Yeast Buns) 187

Part 1

Introduction

Eating properly can be a major challenge of life for those trying to improve their health. When you are hungry and want to fill your stomach with something tasty, the urge to reach for that package of microwavable "substance" can be overwhelming!If you are out and about in the workplace, you are surrounded by restaurants tempting you with delicious meals that have no concern if they make you gain 5 pounds.

All the ingredients are natural with no grains, processed or refined foods allowed. Feel great about your choice and save some money too, when you prepare one of these delicious healthy recipes.

Wholesome Hotcake Breakfast

Prep Time: 5 minutes

Cook Time: 25 minutes

Servings: 2

INGREDIENTS

8 slices nitrate-free bacon

Raw honey, agave nectar or date butter (optional)

Pancakes

1 1/4 cups almond flour

2 cage-free eggs

1/2 cup nut milk

2 tablespoons raw honey (or agave, date butter or stevia)

1 teaspoon baking powder

1 teaspoon vanilla

1/4 teaspoon Celtic sea salt

Coconut oil (for cooking)

Raw, agave or date butter (for garnish, optional)

INSTRUCTIONS

1. Heat large pan or skillet over medium-high heat.

2. Place bacon in hot pan and cook until crisp, about 4 - 5 minutes on each side. Remove bacon from pan and place on paper towel to drain. Reserve bacon fat in pan to cook Pancakes.

3. For Pancakes, in medium mixing bowl, beat eggs, nut milk, sweetener and vanilla with hand mixer or whisk. Add almond flour, salt and baking powder. Beat until smooth.

4. Use ladle or dry measure cup to pour batter onto hot oiled skillet. Fit 3 - 4 pancakes comfortably, so they do not touch as they spread.

5. Cook until edges are firm and batter bubbles slightly, about 3 - 4 minutes.

6. Carefully flip pancakes with spatula and cook for 1 - 2 minutes, or until cooked through. Repeat with remaining batter. Add coconut oil to pan, if necessary.

7. Transfer Pancakes and bacon to serving dish. Top with sweetener of choice and serve immediately.

Great Steak Breakfast

Prep Time: 5 minutes

Cook Time: 20 minutes

Servings: 1

INGREDIENTS

8 oz (1/2 lb) grass-fed bone-in steak (about 1 inch thick)

2 cage-free eggs

Celtic sea salt, to taste

Cracked black pepper, to taste

Coconut oil or bacon fat (for cooking)

INSTRUCTIONS

1. Heat cast iron pan or skillet over medium heat.

2. Sprinkle steak with salt and cracked black pepper on both sides. Place in hot pan and sear about 5 - 7 minutes per side for medium doneness. Flip steak halfway through cooking.

3. Remove steak from hot pan and allow to rest on cutting board or plate for a few minutes.

4. Heat medium pan over medium-high heat. Add 1 heaping tablespoon bacon fat or coconut oil to hot pan.

5. Gently add eggs to hot oiled pan and cover with well fitting lid. Decrease heat to medium-low and let eggs cook about 3 minutes for over-medium doneness.

6. Carefully release eggs from pan with spatula and transfer to serving dish. Top with cracked black pepper, to taste. Transfer rested steak to serving dish and serve hot.

Crispy Chicken And Waffles

Prep Time: 20 minutes

Cook Time: 15 minutes

Servings: 2

INGREDIENTS

Waffles

1 cup almond flour

1/4 coconut flour

3 cage-free eggs (separated)

1/4 cup coconut oil (or coconut or cacao butter, melted)

1/4 cup raw honey (or agave, date butter or stevia)

2 teaspoons aluminum-free baking soda

1 teaspoon vanilla

Pinch Celtic sea salt

Coconut oil (for cooking)

Raw honey, agave, fruit syrup (for garnish, optional)

Chicken Strips

8 oz (1/2 lb) boneless, skinless chicken (white or dark meat)

1 cage-free egg

1/2 cup coarse almond meal (or almond flour)

1 teaspoon flax meal

1/2 teaspoon paprika

1/2 teaspoon ground black pepper

1/2 teaspoon Celtic sea salt

1/4 teaspoon cayenne pepper (optional)

INSTRUCTIONS

1. Preheat waffle iron. Use wadded paper towel to carefully coat cooking surface with coconut oil. Heat medium pan over medium-high heat. Lightly coat pan with coconut oil.
2. For Waffles, in medium mixing bowl, beat egg whites to medium-stiff peaks with hand mixer, about 5 minutes.
3. In small mixing bowl, combine flours, salt and baking soda. In large mixing bowl, beat together egg yolks, oil or butter, sweetener and vanilla with hand mixer or whisk.
4. Beat flour mixture into egg yolk mixture. Gently fold egg whites into egg yolk batter.
5. Pour portion of batter onto hot waffle iron. Do not overfill. Cook 4 - 5 minutes, until golden brown and crisp. Repeat with remaining batter. Set aside cooked Waffles.
7. For Chicken Strips, cut chicken into equal portions. Add almond meal, flax meal, salt spices and to shallow dish and blend.
8. Add egg to separate shallow dish and beat. Dip and coat chicken in beaten egg, then dredge and coat well in almond meal mixture.
9. Carefully place coated chicken in hot oiled pan. Cook until golden brown and cooked through, about 3 - 4 minutes per side, depending on thickness. Turn with tongs halfway through cooking.
10. Remove Chicken Strips from pan and place on paper towel to drain.
11. Transfer cooked Waffles to serving dish. Top with Chicken Strips. Drizzle with raw honey, agave, or your favorite fruit syrup (optional).
12. Serve immediately.

Southern Style Avocado Egg Salad

Prep Time: 5 minutes
Cook Time: 15 minutes
Servings: 4

INGREDIENTS

8 cage-free eggs
1 avocado
1 celery stalk
1/4 sweet onion
1/4 cup sweet pickle relish (or dill pickle relish + 1 tablespoon raw honey, agave or date butter)
1/4 cup organic mustard
2 teaspoons paprika
1/2 teaspoon ground black pepper
1/4 teaspoon Celtic sea salt

INSTRUCTIONS

1. Bring medium pot of lightly salted water to a boil. Leave enough room in pot for eggs.
2. Gently add eggs to hot water with tongs and cook about 10 minutes.
3. Drain eggs into colander in sink. Fill pot with cold water and add eggs back to pot. Let cold water run slowly over eggs in pot to cool.
4. Slice and pit avocado. Scoop flesh into medium mixing bowl. Thinly slice celery. Peel and finely dice onion. Add to mixing bowl with relish, mustard, salt and spices. Mix with large spoon to combine.

5. Crack cooled eggs and peel off shells. Add boiled eggs to medium mixing bowl.

6. Use a fork or knife to chop eggs. Use large spoon to mix and mash ingredients together until smooth mixture with soft chunks forms. Stir to combine.

7. Transfer to serving dish and serve immediately. Or refrigerate about 20 minutes and serve chilled.

Grilled Cashew Cheese Sandwich

Prep Time: 20 minutes*

Cook Time: 60 minutes

Servings: 6

INGREDIENTS

White Bread

1 1/3 cups arrowroot powder

1 1/4 cups almond flour

4 cage-free eggs

4 cage-free egg whites

1/4 cup coconut oil (or cacao or coconut butter, melted)

2 teaspoons apple cider vinegar (or coconut vinegar or aminos)

1 1/2 tablespoons baking powder

1/2 tablespoon Celtic sea salt

Coconut oil (for cooking)

Cheese

1 1/2 cup cashews

1/4 cup nutritional yeast

1 lemon

1/2 teaspoon mustard powder

1/2 teaspoon ground white pepper (or ground black pepper)

1/2 teaspoon Celtic sea salt

Water

INSTRUCTIONS

1. *Soak cashews in enough water to cover for at least 4 hours, or overnight in refrigerator. Drain and rinse.

2. Preheat oven to 350 degrees F. Coat medium loaf pan with coconut oil.

3. For White Bread, in large mixing bowl, beat egg whites with whisk or hand mixer until frothy, about 1 minute. Add eggs, oil and vinegar and beat until light and thickened, about 2 minutes.

4. Sift arrowroot powder, almond flour, baking powder and salt into medium mixing bowl. Slowly stir flour mixture into egg mixture. Mix until well combined.

5. Pour batter into prepared loaf pan and bake for about 40 minutes, or until toothpick inserted into center comes out clean. Remove pan from oven and set aside to cool.

6. For Cheese, juice lemon into food processor or high-speed blender. Add cashews, nutritional yeast, salt and spices to processor. Process until smooth, about 2 minutes. Add enough water to reach thick, smooth consistency. Set aside.

7. Heat large pan over medium heat.

8. Once White Bread is cool slightly, insert knife around edges and remove from pan. Cut of ends of loaf, then cut into 12 slices.

9. Spread oil or butter on one side of each White Bread slice. Spread thick Cheese on bare side of each slice. Place slices together on cheese side.

10. Carefully place each sandwich in hot pan and grill until browned, about 2 - 3 minutes per side.

11. Transfer to serving dish and serve immediately.

Wholly Jalapeño "Cornbread"

Prep Time: 5 minutes
Cook Time: 25 minutes
Servings: 12

INGREDIENTS

1 1/2 cups almond flour
3 cage-free eggs
1/2 cup coconut oil (or coconut or cacao butter, melted) (or sub 1/4 cup with unsweetened applesauce)
1/4 cup nutritional yeast
2 fresh jalapeños (or 1/4 cup pickled jalapeño slices)
2 tablespoons organic apple cider vinegar
2 teaspoons baking powder
1/2 teaspoon paprika
1/2 teaspoon ground turmeric or mustard (optional)
1/2 teaspoon ground white pepper (or ground black pepper)

INSTRUCTIONS

1. Preheat oven to 350 degrees F. Lightly coat baking dish or cast-iron pan with coconut oil.
2. Beat eggs in medium mixing bowl with hand mixer or whisk until thick and slightly frothy. Add oil or butter, nutritional yeast and vinegar. Mix well.
3. Mix in almond meal, baking powder, and spices until combined.
4. Remove stems from fresh jalapenos. Slice and remove seeds. Stir in fresh or pickled jalapeño slices.
5. Pour batter into prepared baking dish or pan and bake 30 -35 minutes, until edges are golden brown and top is firm.

6. Remove from oven. Slice and serve warm. Or allow to cool to temperature and serve.

Real Deal Chili

Prep Time: 5 minutes

Cook Time: 40 minutes

Servings: 4

INGREDIENTS

16 oz (1 lb) lean grass-fed ground beef (or elk, bison, turkey or chicken)

15 oz (1 can) organic tomato sauce

29 oz (2 cans) organic diced tomatoes

1 cup water

1 cup cashews

1 small onion

1 bell pepper

2 cloves garlic

2 tablespoons chili powder

1 1/2 tablespoons smoked paprika (or paprika)

1 tablespoon ground cumin

1 teaspoon Mexican oregano (or dried oregano)

1 teaspoon ground black pepper

1/2 teaspoon cayenne pepper

1 teaspoon Celtic sea salt

1 tablespoon coconut oil

INSTRUCTIONS

1. Heat medium pot over medium-high heat. Add 1 tablespoon coconut oil to hot pan.

2. Peel onion and garlic. Remove stems, seeds and veins from bell pepper. Roughly chop and add to food processor or high-speed blender. Pulse until finely minced.

3. Add minced veggies to hot skillet and sauté for about 1 minute. Add ground beef and spices. Brown beef for about 5 minutes. Stir with whisk to break up meat well, or wooden spoon to keep beef chunkier.

4. Add whole cans of diced tomatoes and tomato sauce, and water. Stir to combine.

5. Bring to a simmer, then reduce heat to medium and cover pot loosely with lid to prevent splatter. Simmer about 30 minutes. Stir occasionally.

6. Remove from heat and transfer to serving dish. Use large serving spoon or ladle to serve hot.

Easy Cheesy Fries

Prep Time: 10 minutes*

Cook Time: 35 minutes

Servings: 2

INGREDIENTS

Sweet Potato Fries

1 large sweet potato

2 tablespoons coconut oil

1/2 teaspoon smoked paprika

1/2 teaspoon ground black pepper

1/2 teaspoon Celtic sea salt

Coconut oil (for cooking)

Cheese Sauce

3/4 cup cashews

2 tablespoons nutritional yeast

1/2 lemon

1/4 teaspoon mustard powder

1/4 teaspoon cayenne pepper

1/4 teaspoon ground white pepper (or ground black pepper)

1/4 teaspoon Celtic sea salt

Water

INSTRUCTIONS

1. *Soak cashews in enough water to cover for at least 4 hours, or overnight in refrigerator. Drain and rinse.

2. Preheat oven to 450 degrees F. Line sheet pan with parchment or coat lightly with coconut oil.

3. For Sweet Potato Fries, peel sweet potato if preferred, but do not rinse. Slice sweet potato into 1/4 inch sticks and add to medium mixing bowl with coconut oil and spices. Toss to coat.

4. Spread potatoes in well-spaced, single layer on prepared sheet pan. Sprinkle salt evenly over potatoes and bake for 10 minutes.

5. Carefully remove sheet pan from oven and turn fries over with tongs or spatula. Back another 10 minutes, or until golden and crispy.

6. For Cheese Sauce, juice lemon into food processor or high-speed blender. Add cashews, nutritional yeast, salt and spices to processor. Process until smooth, about 2 minutes. Add enough water to reach desired consistency. Transfer to serving dish.

7. Remove Sweet Potato Fries from oven and transfer to serving dish. Serve immediately with Cheese Sauce.

Stacked Portobello Burger

Prep Time: 10 minutes
Cook Time: 35 minutes
Servings: 2

INGREDIENTS

4 large Portobello mushroom caps
12 oz grass-fed ground beef (or chicken, turkey, bison, elk, etc.)
1/2 white onion
Cracked black pepper, to taste
Celtic sea salt, to taste
Coconut oil (for cooking)

Portobello Cheese Sauce
4 Portobello stems
3/4 cup cashews
2 tablespoons nutritional yeast
1/2 lemon
1/4 teaspoon mustard powder
1/4 teaspoon ground white pepper (or ground black pepper)
1/4 teaspoon Celtic sea salt
Water
Bacon fat or coconut oil (for cooking)

INSTRUCTIONS

1. *Soak cashews in enough water to cover for at least 4 hours, or overnight in refrigerator. Drain and rinse.

2. Preheat oven to 450 degrees F. Heat small pan over medium heat. Add 1 tablespoon bacon fat or coconut oil to hot pan. Line sheet pan with aluminum foil. Place metal cooling or baking rack over lined sheet pan.

3. Remove stems from Portobello mushroom caps. Chop and reserve stems. Place mushroom caps gill-side up on prepared sheet pan. Drizzle caps lightly with coconut oil.

4. Peel onion and slice crosswise into 2 full 1/4 inch cross sections. Keep rings intact and place on prepared sheet pan. Drizzle slightly with coconut oil and sprinkle with salt and pepper.

5. Form ground beef into 3/4 inch patties. Place on prepared sheet pan and sprinkle with salt and pepper.

6. Bake about 12 minutes, for medium-well burgers. Remove from oven and sprinkle mushroom caps with salt and pepper.

7. For Portobello Cheese Sauce, add chopped mushrooms stems to hot oiled pan. Sauté until soft and lightly caramelized, about 5 minutes. Stir occasionally.

8. Juice lemon into food processor or high-speed blender. Add cashews, nutritional yeast, salt and spices to processor. Process until smooth, about 2 minutes. Add enough water to reach desired consistency.

9. Add mixture to sautéed mushrooms and stir to heat Portobello Cheese Sauce through, about 2 minutes. Remove from heat.

10. Transfer 2 mushroom caps to serving dish, gill-side up. Top with roasted onion ring slice, then hamburger patty. Spoon Portobello Cheese Sauce over patty and top with remaining Portobello caps, gill-side down.

11. Serve hot.

Zesty Meatball Marinara

Prep Time: 5 minutes

Cook Time: 20 minutes

Servings: 4

INGREDIENTS

Meatballs

16 oz (1 lb) lean ground meat (beef, pork, chicken, turkey, bison, or any combination)

3/4 cup almond flour

1 cage-free egg

1/2 small onion (white, yellow or red)

1/2 teaspoon garlic powder

1/2 teaspoon cayenne pepper

1 teaspoon dried parsley

1 teaspoon dried oregano

1 teaspoon paprika

1 teaspoon red pepper flakes

1 teaspoon ground black pepper

1 teaspoon Celtic sea salt

1 tablespoon coconut oil

1 sprig fresh basil (for garnish, optional)

Tomato Sauce

14.5 oz (1 can) organic diced tomatoes

8 oz (1 can) organic tomato sauce

1 garlic clove

1/2 teaspoon dried oregano

1/2 teaspoon dried basil

1/2 teaspoon red pepper flakes

1/2 teaspoon ground black pepper

1 teaspoon coconut oil

INSTRUCTIONS

1. Heat large pan over medium heat. Add 1 tablespoon coconut oil to hot pan. Heat medium saucepan over medium heat. Add 1 teaspoon coconut oil.

2. For Tomato Sauce, peel garlic and mince. Add to medium saucepan and sauté until just golden, about 30 seconds. Add diced tomatoes, tomato sauce, salt and spices. Simmer about 5 - 10 minutes, stirring occasionally.

3. For Meatballs, peel onion process in food processor or high-speed blender, or finely grate.

4. Add to large mixing bowl. Add egg, ground meat, almond flour, spices and salt. Mix well with hands or large wooden spoon.

5. Form 24 meatballs with scoop or tablespoon, then roll in hands. Add meatballs to hot large pan and brown for 10 minutes. Turn with spatula or tongs to cook on all sides.

6. Add Meatballs to Tomato Sauce and simmer another 5 minutes.

7. Transfer Meatballs to serving dish. Top with simmering Tomato Sauce. Garnish with fresh basil (optional).

8. Serve hot.

Delicious Eggplant Parmesan

Prep Time: 10 minutes

Cook Time: 20 minutes

Servings: 4

INGREDIENTS

Eggplant

1 eggplant

2 cage-free eggs

1 1/2 cups almond flour

1 tablespoon garlic powder

1 teaspoon dried oregano

1/2 teaspoon dried parsley

Celtic sea salt, to taste

Ground black pepper, to taste

1 small sprig fresh basil (for garnish)

Coconut oil (for cooking)

Pasta Sauce

14.5 oz (1 can) organic diced tomatoes

8 oz (1 can) organic tomato sauce

2 garlic cloves

1 tablespoon oregano (dried or fresh)

1 teaspoons paprika

1 teaspoon ground black pepper

1/2 teaspoon Celtic sea salt

1 teaspoon coconut oil

Almond Parmesan

1 cup almonds

2 tablespoons nutritional yeast

1 teaspoon garlic powder
1/2 teaspoon Celtic sea salt

INSTRUCTIONS

1. Heat medium saucepan over medium heat. Add 1 teaspoon coconut oil to hot pan. Heat large pan over medium-high heat. Coat hot pan well with coconut oil.

2. For Pasta Sauce, peel and mince garlic, then add to medium pan. Sauté until golden and aromatic, about 1 minute. Then add diced tomatoes, tomato sauce, salt and spices. Simmer until sauce reduces to desired consistency, about 5 - 10 minutes. Stir occasionally, then remove from heat and set aside.

3. For Eggplant, sift almond flour and spices into shallow dish. Add eggs to small shallow bowl and whisk.

4. Cut eggplant crosswise into 1/3 inch disks. Sprinkle with salt and pepper. Dredge eggplant in almond mixture until well coated. Shake off excess flour, then dip in egg. Return to almond flour mixture, then carefully place in large hot oiled pan. Repeat until pan is full, but not crowded.

5. Pan-fry eggplant until golden brown, about 2 minutes on each side. Flip halfway through cooking. Transfer breaded eggplant to paper towels to drain. Repeat with remaining eggplant.

6. For Almond Parmesan, add all ingredients to food processor or high-speed blender. Process until desired consistency is reached, coarsely or finely ground. Set aside.

7. Transfer breaded eggplant to serving dishes. To assemble, place layer of eggplant on serving dish. Spoon layer of Pasta Sauce over eggplant. Sprinkle on Almond Parmesan. Repeat with two more layers each of Eggplant, Pasta Sauce and Almond Parmesan.

8. Remove basil leaves from stem, stack together, roll up tightly, the thinly slice crosswise. Top dish with extra Almond Parmesan and chiffon of fresh basil.

9. Serve hot.

Zucchini Pasta Lasagna

Prep Time: 20 minutes

Cook Time: 40 minutes

Servings: 4

INGREDIENTS

1 large zucchini

Meat Filling

8 oz (1/2 lb) lean ground meat (beef, pork, turkey, chicken, etc.)

1/4 small onion (white, yellow or red)

1 teaspoon dried oregano

1/2 teaspoon garlic powder

1/2 teaspoon dried basil

1/2 teaspoon ground black pepper

1/2 teaspoon Celtic sea salt

Tomato Sauce

6 oz (1 can) organic tomato paste

8 oz (1 can) organic tomato sauce

2 teaspoons dried oregano

1 teaspoon garlic powder

1/2 teaspoon paprika

1/2 teaspoon ground black pepper

1/2 teaspoon Celtic sea salt

Spinach Ricotta

2 cup cashews

1 cup frozen chopped spinach (thawed)

1 teaspoon ground white pepper (or black pepper)

1/2 teaspoon garlic powder

1/2 teaspoon onion powder

1/2 teaspoon dried basil
1/2 teaspoon Celtic sea salt
Water

INSTRUCTIONS

1. *Soak cashews in enough water to cover for at least 4 hours, or overnight in refrigerator. Drain and rinse.

2. Preheat oven to 350 degrees F. Heat medium pan over medium-high heat.

3. For Meat Filling, peel onion and grate or mince. Add to hot pan with ground meat, salt and spices. Sauté until meat is browned, about 5 - 8 minutes. Remove from heat and set aside.

4. For Spinach Ricotta, add soaked cashews, salt and spices to food processor or high-speed blender. Process until smooth, about 2 minutes. Add chopped spinach and pulse to incorporate. Set aside.

5. For Pasta Sauce, add all ingredients to medium mixing bowl and mix until combined. Set aside.

6. Slice zucchini lengthwise into 1/4 inch slices with mandolin or knife.

7. To assemble, layer a few spoonfuls of Tomato Sauce along bottom of baking dish. Top with layer of zucchini, Spinach Ricotta, Meat Filling and Sauce. Repeat process with remaining components. End with a layer of zucchini, then Sauce on top. Add a dash of extra spices, if preferred.

8. Place Lasagna in oven and bake for about 40 minutes, until heated through. Remove from oven and let cool about 10 minutes.

9. Serve warm.

Sautéed Sausage And Peppers

Prep Time: 5 minutes

Cook Time: 20 minutes

Servings: 4

INGREDIENTS

4 large spicy Italian sausage links (pork, chicken or turkey)

1 yellow onion

1 green bell pepper

Cracked black pepper, to taste

INSTRUCTIONS

1. Heat large cast iron pan or skillet over medium heat.

2. Add sausage links to hot pan and sear on one side about 8 - 10 minutes.

3. Peel onion. Remove stems, seeds and veins from bell pepper. Chop or slice onion and pepper and add to pan.

4. Turn over sausage links and stir veggies. Sear sausage and sauté veggies until sausage is cooked through and veggies are tender and caramelized, about 8 - 10 minutes. Stir veggies around sausage occasionally. Try not to disturb sausage too much.

5. Transfer sausage to cutting board and slice into 1 1/2 inch pieces, if desired.

6. Transfer Sausage and Peppers to serving dish and serve hot.

Mac And "Cheese" Please

Prep Time: 15 minutes
Cook Time: 30 minutes
Servings: 4
INGREDIENTS
2 spaghetti squash (or summer squash or zucchini)
Cheese Sauce
1 1/2 cup cashews
1/4 cup nutritional yeast
1 lemon
1/4 teaspoon cayenne pepper
1/2 teaspoon mustard powder
1/2 teaspoon ground white pepper (or ground black pepper)
1/2 teaspoon Celtic sea salt
Water
Topping
1 cup almonds
2 tablespoons nutritional yeast
1/2 teaspoon mustard powder
1/2 teaspoon Celtic sea salt
Pinch cayenne pepper
INSTRUCTIONS
1. *Soak cashews in enough water to cover for at least 4 hours, or overnight in refrigerator. Drain and rinse.
2. Preheat oven to 350 degrees F. Bring large pot of salted water to boil over high heat.

3. Gently place squash into boiling water and cook until tender, about 15 minutes. Remove and submerge in cool water to cool. Set aside.

4. For Cheese Sauce, juice lemon into food processor or high-speed blender. Add cashews, nutritional yeast, salt and spices to processor. Process until smooth, about 2 minutes. Add enough water to reach desired consistency. Transfer to medium mixing bowl.

5. For Topping, add all ingredients to clean food processor or high-speed blender. Process to reach desired consistency. Mixture should be coarsely or finely ground. Set aside.

6. Remove seeds from cooled spaghetti squash, and use fork to shred. Or grate, julienne (thinly slice) or spiralize summer squash or zucchini. Add squash Cheese Sauce in mixing bowl. Gently mix to combine.

7. Transfer mixture to baking dish. Sprinkle Topping over dish.

8. Place in oven and bake for about 10 - 15 minutes, until heated through.

9. Remove from oven and serve warm.

Winter's Night Chicken Pie

Prep Time: 25 minutes*

Cook Time: 45 minutes

Servings: 4

INGREDIENTS

Filling

16oz (1lb) boneless skin-on chicken (or pheasant, game hen, etc.)

2 cups chicken broth

2 large carrots

1 large celery stalk

1 green bell pepper

1 small onion

2 garlic cloves

1/2 lemon

1 cage-free egg

2 tablespoons tapioca flour

2 tablespoons coconut flour

2 teaspoons dried thyme (or 4 teaspoons fresh thyme)

1/2 teaspoon black pepper

Celtic sea salt (to taste)

Bacon fat or coconut oil (for cooking)

Crust

1 1/2 cup almond flour

1/2 cup coconut flour

3/4 cup cold coconut oil (or room temperature cacao butter)

3 cage-free eggs

2 teaspoons dried thyme

1 teaspoon Celtic sea salt

Water

INSTRUCTIONS

1. *For Crust, add almond and coconut flour, thyme and salt to medium mixing bowl. Cut oil or butter into flour with fork until crumbly. Mix in eggs until dough starts to combine together. Mix in enough water to bring together tender dough.

2. *Divide dough in half and roll into round disks. Place one dough round over pie pan or plate and gentle press in. Cover and place in freezer 1 hour. Cover and refrigerate remaining dough.

3. Preheat oven to 350 degrees F. Heat large pot over medium heat.

4. For Filling, add 2 tablespoons bacon fat or coconut oil to hot pot. Add chicken pieces skin-side down. Cook chicken until browned and fat renders out, about 5 minutes. Turn chicken over and continue cooking another 5 minutes. Remove chicken from pot and set aside.

5. Add coconut and tapioca flour to pot and whisk until smooth paste forms. Gradually whisk in chicken broth. Simmer about 5 minutes, whisking occasionally.

6. Peel and mince garlic. Peel onion and dice. Remove stems, seeds and veins from bell pepper, then chop. Dice carrots and celery. Add veggies to pot with thyme, salt, pepper and lemon juice.

7. Remove skin from par-cooked chicken and chop. Add back to pot.

8. Beat egg in small mixing bowl and slowly spoon in hot chicken stock to temper. Once egg is tempered, add to pot and stir to

incorporate. Simmer for 10 minutes, then remove from heat and set aside.

9. Remove Crust from freezer and refrigerator. Carefully ladle Filling into bottom frozen Crust. Lay top Crust over Filling. Pinch together and crimp edges of top and bottom Crust to seal.

10. Brush top Crust with bacon fat or coconut oil and sprinkle with salt. Use knife to cut a few slits in top Crust.

11. Bake for 35 - 45 minutes, or until crust is golden. Remove from oven and let to cool at least 15 minutes.

12. Serve warm.

1ˢᵗ Prize Sheppard's Pie

Prep Time: 20 minutes

Cook Time: 60 minutes

Servings: 4

INGREDIENTS

Meat Filling

24 oz (1 1/2 lbs) grass-fed ground lamb (or beef, bison, elk, etc.)

1 cup chicken broth or stock (or beef brother or stock, or red wine)

1 large onion (yellow or white)

2 carrots

6 - 10 asparagus stalks (about 1/2 cup chopped)

1/2 sweet potato (about 1/2 cup diced)

2 garlic cloves

1 tablespoon organic tomato paste

1 teaspoon tamari (or coconut aminos)

2 tablespoons tapioca flour (or arrow root powder)

1 sprig fresh rosemary

1 sprig fresh thyme

1/2 teaspoon ground black pepper (or ground white pepper)

1 teaspoon Celtic sea salt

Bacon fat or coconut oil (for cooking)

Parsnip Topping

4 medium parsnips

1/2 medium onion (yellow or white)

2 tablespoons cacao butter (or coconut oil)

2 cups water

3/4 teaspoon Celtic sea salt

1/2 ground white pepper (or ground black pepper) (optional)

INSTRUCTIONS

1. Heat medium pot over medium heat. Add 2 tablespoons bacon fat or coconut oil to hot pot.
2. For Meat Filling, peel and mince garlic. Peel and chop onion. Dice carrots and sweet potato. Chop asparagus. Add to hot oiled pot and sauté about 5 minutes.
3. Add lamb, salt and spices to veggies. Brown lamb and sauté another 5 minutes. Whisk in tapioca flour and cook another minute.
4. Remove rosemary and thymes leaves from stems and add to pot with stock, tomato paste and tamari. Let simmer and thicken about 12 minutes.
5. Preheat oven to 400 degrees F. Heat large pan with lid over medium heat. Add butter or oil to hot pan.
6. For Parsnip Topping, peel and mince or finely grate onion. Add to hot pan and sauté until translucent and aromatic, about 2 minutes.
7. Peel and slice or chop parsnips. Add to onions with water. Increase heat to high and bring to a simmer. Cover pan loosely with lid. Cook parsnips partially covered until softened and most of the water has evaporated, about 10 minutes.
8. Pour parsnips and onions into food processor or high-speed blender. Process until thick, smooth mixture forms. Add enough water to reach desired consistency. Set aside.
9. Transfer Meat Filling to baking or casserole dish. Top with Parsnip Topping. Smooth over or create design with offset spatula or back of spoon.
10. Bake about 25 minutes, until Parsnip Topping is golden.

11. Remove from oven and let cool at least 10 minutes. Serve warm.

Southern Chicken And Dumplings

Prep Time: 10 minutes

Cook Time: 40 minutes

Servings: 4

INGREDIENTS

Chicken Soup

16 oz (1 lb) skin-on bone-in chicken pieces

3 cups organic chicken broth or stock

3 cups water

2 carrots

2 celery stalks

1/2 small white onion

2 bay leaves

2 teaspoons dried thyme (or 4 teaspoons fresh thyme)

1/2 teaspoon paprika

1 teaspoon black pepper

1 teaspoon Celtic sea salt

Dumplings

1 1/2 cups almond flour

1/4 cup arrowroot powder

1 cage-free egg

1/4 cup chilled coconut oil (or room temperature coconut or cacao butter)

1/2 teaspoon baking soda

1/2 ground bay leaf

1/2 teaspoon garlic powder

1/2 teaspoon ground white pepper (or ground black pepper)

1/2 teaspoon Celtic sea salt

Nut milk or chicken broth or stock

INSTRUCTIONS

1. Heat large pot over medium-high heat. Place chicken skin-side down in hot pot. Sear and render out fat for about 5 minutes.

2. Chop carrots and celery. Peel onion and mince. Add veggies to chicken with salt and pepper.

3. Turn chicken over and brown on flesh side about 5 minutes. Stir veggies occasionally.

4. Add bay, thyme and paprika, chicken stock and water to pot. Increase heat to high and bring to a boil. Reduce heat and simmer about 25 minutes. Place lid loosely over pot to prevent splatter, if necessary.

5. For Dumplings, sift almond flour and arrowroot into medium mixing bowl. Cut in solid oil or butter with fork until crumbly mixture forms. Add egg, salt and spices, baking soda, and enough nut milk or chicken broth to bring together soft, slightly sticky dough.

6. Use tablespoon or small scoop to gently drop dough into Chicken Soup. Cover with well fitting lid and let simmer about 10 minutes.

7. Gently stir soup to prevent Dumplings from sticking. Turn over any Dumplings that are not submerged. Continue simmering 5 minutes, or until Dumplings are cooked through.

8. Remove from heat and transfer to serving dish. Use large serving spoon or ladle to serve hot.

Crunch-Fried Steak And Gravy

Prep Time: 10 minutes

Cook Time: 15 minutes

Servings: 2

INGREDIENTS

Country Fried Steak

12 oz (3/4 lb) grass-fed beef (cube steak or fillet)

1 cage-free egg

1 teaspoon coconut aminos (or tamari)

1/3 cup arrowroot powder

1/4 cup macadamia nuts

1/4 cup pistachios (or almonds or cashews)

1/4 teaspoon garlic powder

1/4 teaspoon onion powder

1/4 teaspoon paprika

1/4 teaspoon cracked black pepper (or ground black pepper)

1/4 teaspoon Celtic sea salt

Pinch cayenne pepper

Pinch dried oregano

Coconut oil (for cooking)

Bacon fat (for cooking)

White Gravy

2 teaspoons arrowroot powder

5 oz (1/2 can) full-fat coconut milk

1/2 teaspoon Celtic salt

1/2 teaspoon ground white pepper (or ground black pepper)

Bacon fat

INSTRUCTIONS

1. Heat cast iron pan or skillet over medium-high heat. Add 1 tablespoon each bacon fat and coconut oil to hot pan.
2. For Country Fried Steak, add nuts to food processor or high-speed blender. Process until finely ground. Add arrowroot, salt and spices. Pulse to incorporated. Transfer mixture to shallow dish. Set aside.
3. In separate shallow dish, beat egg and coconut aminos. Set aside.
4. Tenderize beef fillet with tenderizing mallet, if using. Dip and coat cube steak in egg mixture, then dredge and coat well in nut mixture.
5. Place coated cube steak into hot oiled pan. Cook until golden and crisp, about 2 minutes on each side. Repeat with remaining steak. Remove cooked steak from pan and place on paper towel to drain.
6. For White Gravy, add enough bacon fat to hot skillet so there is about 2 - 3 tablespoons in pan. Allow to heat thoroughly.
7. Add arrowroot to pan. Whisk and cook for 1 minute. Whisk in coconut milk. Whisk and cook another minute. Whisk in salt and pepper. Remove from heat.
8. Transfer Country Fried Steak to serving dish. Top with White Gravy and serve hot.

Liver And Caramelized Onions

Prep Time: 20 minutes*
Cook Time: 25 minutes
Servings: 4
INSTRUCTIONS

20 oz (1 1/4 lb) calves liver

2 onions (yellow or white)

4 slices nitrate-free bacon

1 lemon

2 tablespoons arrowroot powder

1/2 teaspoon Celtic sea salt

1/2 teaspoon cracked black pepper (or ground black pepper)

Bacon fat or coconut oil (for cooking)

INSTRUCTIONS

1. *Remove thin outer membrane from liver and slice into 1/4 inch fillets. Add to glass container. Juice lemon into container and toss to coat. Cover well and refrigerate overnight.

2. Heat large cast-iron pan or skillet set over medium heat.

3. Cut bacon lengthwise into long, thin strips. Then cut in thirds crosswise and add to hot pan. Sauté bacon and let crisp, about 5 minutes. Stir occasionally. Decrease heat to medium-low.

4. Peel and thinly slice onions. Add to bacon and sauté until caramelized, about 10 minutes. Stir occasionally. Remove caramelized onions and bacon from pan and set aside.

5. Drain liver fillets in colander in sink. Rinse under running water, then pat dry.

6. In shallow dish, add arrowroot powder, salt and pepper. Mix with fork to combine.

7. Dredge liver slices in arrowroot mixture and shake off excess. Place coated liver fillets on a plate and coat remaining liver fillets.

8. Add 2 tablespoons bacon fat or coconut oil to hot pan. Add single layer of coated liver to hot oiled pan and sear for 1 minute per side. Place liver on paper towel to drain. Repeat with remaining liver.

9. Transfer liver to serving dish. Top with caramelized onions and bacon. Serve immediately .

Breaded Baked Chicken

Prep Time: 10 minutes
Cook Time: 60 minutes
Servings: 4

INGREDIENTS

32 oz (2 lb) bone-in, skinless chicken
3/4 cup fine almond flour
3/4 cup coarse almond meal (or almond flour)
2 cage free eggs
1/3 cup nut milk
1/2 teaspoon cayenne pepper
1 teaspoon ground black pepper
1 1/2 teaspoons paprika
1 1/2 tablespoons Celtic sea salt
Coconut oil (in spray bottle)

INSTRUCTIONS

1. Preheat oven to 350 degrees F. Fill spray bottle with warm coconut oil.

2. Line sheet pan with aluminum foil. Place metal cooling or baking rack over lined sheet pan. Generously spray metal rack with coconut oil to coat. Set second sheet pan aside.

3. Add almond meal and/or flour to small mixing bowl with 1 tablespoon salt and spices. Mix to combine with fork or whisk to break up clumps.

4. In shallow dish, beat eggs and nut milk until combined.

5. Use serving spoon or measuring cup to dust second sheet pan with layer of almond flour mixture onto. Sprinkle chicken with 1/2 tablespoon salt.

6. Dip and coat all chicken pieces in egg mixture then lay on second sheet pan, over layer of almond flour mixture. Use spoon or measuring cut to sprinkle almond flour mixture from mixing bowl over dipped chicken. Pat almond flour mixture into chicken on all sides until well coated.

7. Transfer coasted chicken to prepared wire rack. Generously spray coated chicken with coconut oil.

8. Bake 60 - 70 minutes, until coating is crisp and chicken is cooked through. Remove from oven and allow to cool at least 10 minutes. Then place crispy chicken on paper towels to drain, if desired.

9. Transfer to serving dish and serve immediately.

Garlic Parsnip Mash

Prep Time: 10 minutes
Cook Time: 20 minutes
Servings: 4
INSTRUCTIONS

4 medium parsnips

1/2 white onion

4 garlic cloves

Celtic sea salt (to taste)

Ground black pepper (to taste)

Water

Bacon fat or coconut oil (for cooking)

INSTRUCTIONS

1. Heat large pan with lid over medium heat. Add 2 tablespoons bacon fat or coconut oil to hot pan.

2. Peel and mince or finely grate onion and garlic. Add to hot oiled pan and sauté until golden and aromatic, about 2 minutes.

3. Peel and slice or chop parsnips. Add to pan with 2 cups water. Increase heat to high and bring to a simmer. Cover pan loosely with lid. Cook partially covered until parsnips soften and most of the water has evaporated, about 10 minutes.

4. Pour parsnips, onions and garlic into food processor or high-speed blender. Process until thick, smooth mixture forms.

5. Transfer to serving dish and serve immediately.

Cheesy Croquettes

Prep Time: 25 minutes*

Cook Time: 60 minutes

Servings: 8

INGREDIENTS

White Bread

1 1/3 cups arrowroot powder

1 1/4 cups almond flour

4 cage-free eggs

4 cage-free egg whites

1/4 cup coconut oil (or cacao or coconut butter, melted)

2 teaspoons apple cider vinegar (or coconut vinegar or aminos)

1 1/2 tablespoons baking powder

1/2 tablespoon Celtic sea salt

Chilled coconut oil (or room temperature coconut or cacao butter, for cooking)

Cheesy Filling

1/2 cup chopped cooked ham (or chicken, turkey, etc.)

4 slices nitrate-free bacon

1/2 onion (white, yellow or red)

3/4 cup cashews

1/4 cup nutritional yeast

1 lemon

1/2 teaspoon mustard powder

1/2 teaspoon cayenne pepper

1/2 teaspoon ground white pepper (or ground black pepper)

1/2 teaspoon Celtic sea salt

Water

INSTRUCTIONS

1. *Soak cashews in enough water to cover for at least 4 hours, or overnight in refrigerator. Drain and rinse.

2. Preheat oven to 350 degrees F. Coat baking dish with coconut oil.

3. For White Bread, in large mixing bowl, beat egg whites with whisk or hand mixer until frothy, about 1 minute. Add eggs, oil and vinegar and beat until light and thickened, about 2 minutes.

4. Sift arrowroot powder, almond flour, baking powder and salt into medium mixing bowl. Slowly stir flour mixture into egg mixture. Mix until well combined.

5. Pour batter into prepared baking pan and bake for about 30 minutes, or until toothpick inserted into center comes out clean. Remove pan from oven and set aside to cool.

6. Heat medium pan over medium-high heat. Line sheet pan with aluminum foil. Place metal cooling or baking rack over lined sheet pan. Generously spray metal rack with coconut oil to coat.

7. For Cheesy Filling, chop bacon and add to hot pan. Sauté until crisp and fat is rendered out, about 8 minutes. Transfer bacon to medium mixing bowl. Reserve bacon fat in pan.

8. Peel and mince or finely grate onion. Add to hot oiled pan and sauté until translucent and aromatic, about 5 minutes.

9. Add chopped, cooked meat to pan and sauté until warm, about 2 minutes. Remove from heat and add to mixing bowl.

10. Juice lemon into food processor or high-speed blender. Add cashews, nutritional yeast, salt and spices to processor. Process until smooth, about 2 minutes. Add enough water to reach desired consistency. Add to mixing bowl.

11. Remove White Bread from baking dish. Cut in half. Dice one portion. Add to Cheesy Filling and mix to combine. Mixture should be moist and stick together when pressed. Add nut milk or water to reach desired consistency, if necessary.

12. Form mixture into golf ball-sized rounds and place on plate.

13. Chop remaining White Bread and add to clean food processor high-speed blender. Pulse to coarsely grind and add to empty mixing bowl. Roll Cheesy Filling balls in ground White Bread. Pat to secure coating and transfer to prepared wire rack. Spray Croquettes with coconut oil.

14. Bake about 20 minutes, until outside is golden brown and crisp. Remove from oven and transfer to serving dish.

15. Serve hot.

Classic Beef Patty

Prep Time: 25 minutes

Cook Time: 30 minutes

Servings: 4

INSTRUCTIONS

Crust

2 cups almond flour

2 cage-free eggs

3 tablespoons chilled coconut oil (or room temperature coconut or cacao butter)

1 teaspoon turmeric

1/4 teaspoon baking soda

1/2 teaspoon Celtic sea salt

Filling

12 oz (3/4 lb) grass-fed beef (ground or fillet)

1/2 small onion (yellow, white or red)

1 tablespoon tamari (or coconut aminos)

1 tablespoon raw honey (or agave or date butter)

1 tablespoon curry powder

1 teaspoon allspice

1 teaspoon chili powder

1 teaspoon red pepper flake

1/2 teaspoon garlic powder

1/2 teaspoon onion powder

1/2 teaspoon Celtic sea salt

INSTRUCTIONS

1. For Crust, sift almond flour into medium mixing bowl. Add baking soda, turmeric and salt.

2. Whisk eggs in small mixing bowl, then add to flour and combine. Slowly cut in coconut oil with fork until malleable dough comes together.

3. Roll dough in plastic wrap or wrap tightly in parchment and refrigerate for 15 minutes.

4. Preheat oven to 400 degrees F. Line sheet pan with parchment or baking mat. Cover cutting board with parchment. Heat medium pan over medium heat.

5. For Filling, grind or mince beef fillet, if using. Peel and mince or finely grate onion. Add onion and beef to hot pan with salt and spices. Sauté until beef is browned and onions are soft, about 8 minutes. Use whisk to break up meat well, or wooden spoon to keep chunkier form. Remove from heat and set aside.

6. Remove dough from refrigerator and divide into 4 portions. Roll dough into balls and use hands to flatten on prepared cutting board. Roll into circles about 1/8 inch thick with rolling pin.

7. Scoop equal portions of Filling into center of one half of dough circle. Fold bare half of dough over filled half. Press edges together, letting any trapped air escape. Crimp edges of dough together with fork. Repeat with remaining dough.

8. Arrange patties on lined sheet pan and bake 15 - 20 minutes, until dough is golden and cooked through. Remove from oven transfer to serving dish.

9. Serve hot.

Ripe Banana Bread

Prep Time: 5 minutes

Cook Time: 40 minutes

Servings: 8

INGREDIENTS

1 cup almond flour

1/4 cup coconut flour

2 overripe bananas

2 cage-free eggs

1/4 cup raw honey (or agave, date butter or stevia)

1/4 cup coconut oil (or coconut or cacao butter, melted) (or unsweetened applesauce or nut butter)

1 tablespoon baking powder

2 teaspoons ground cinnamon

1/2 teaspoon ground nutmeg

1 teaspoon vanilla

1/2 teaspoon Celtic sea salt

INSTRUCTIONS

1. Preheat oven to 350 degrees F. Coat small or medium loaf pan with coconut oil.

2. Peel bananas and add to medium mixing bowl. Beat with hand mixer or whisk. Add eggs, oil or butter, and sweetener. Beat well, about 1 - 2 minutes.

3. In separate bowl, blend flours, baking powder, salt and spices. Pour banana mixture into flour mixture and stir to combine.

4. Pour batter into prepared loaf pan and bake for 30 - 40 minutes, or until browned and firm in the center.

5. Remove from oven and set aside to cool.

6. Slice and serve warm. Or allow to cool completely and serve room temperature.

Natural Pumpkin Bread

Prep Time: 5 minutes

Cook Time: 40 minutes

Servings: 8

INGREDIENTS

1 cup almond flour

3/4 cup coconut flour

15 oz (1 can) pumpkin puree

2 cage-free eggs

1/2 cup nut milk

1/2 cup unsweetened applesauce

1/4 cup coconut oil (or coconut or cacao butter, melted) (or nut butter)

1/4 cup raw honey (or agave, date butter or stevia)

1/4 cup pumpkin seeds

2 teaspoons baking soda

1 tablespoon ground cinnamon

1 teaspoon ground nutmeg

1 teaspoon Celtic sea salt

1/2 teaspoon ground black pepper (optional)

Coconut oil (for cooking)

INSTRUCTIONS

1. Preheat oven to 350 degrees F. Coat medium loaf pan with coconut oil.

2. Add eggs, oil or butter, applesauce, nut milk and sweetener to food processor or high-speed blender. Process until thick and light, about 1 - 2 minutes.

3. Add pumpkin, salt and spices. Process to incorporate.

4. Add flour and baking soda to small mixing bowl and stir to combine. Add to processor in batches and process until well combined.

5. Pour batter into prepared loaf pan and bake 35 - 40 minutes, until firm but springy in the center.

6. Remove from oven and set aside to cool.

7. Slice and serve warm. Or allow to cool completely and serve room temperature.

Part 2

1. Recipe Index

1.1. Appetizers

1) Bibbeliskäs (Cottage cheese with onions and herbs)
2) Bayerische Brezen (Bavarian Pretzels)
3) Gebackener Camembert (Baked Camembert with Red Currant Sauce)
4) Obatzter (Bavarian cheese spread)
5) Markklößchensuppe (Marrow dumplings in Double Consomme)
6) Badischer Wurstsalat (Bologna salad from Baden)
7) Bayerischer Krautsalat (Bavarian cabbage salad)
8) Käsedip (quick cheesedip)
9) Sauerkaut-Schinken Bällchen (Kraut ham balls)
10) Rindfleisch Zwiebel Strudel (Beef onion strudel)
11) Strammer Max (Hearty german sandwich with egg)
12) Speckbrötchen (Smoked ham rolls)
13) Flammkuchen (Onion flatbread with bacon)
14) Heringssalat (Herring salad)
15) Gefüllte Tomaten mit Shrimps (Shrimp stuffed tomatoes)

1.2. Soups

1) Gaisburger Marsch   (Beef & Vegetable Stew with Spätzle)
2) Leberknödelsuppe   (Liver Dumpling Soup)
3) Zwiebelsuppe mit dunklem Bier (Dark Beer Onion Soup)
4) Bier Käse Suppe (Cheese Soup with German Lager)

5) Flädlesuppe (Broth with Strips of Pancake)

6) Pichelsteiner Topf (Pichelsteiner Stew)

7) Ochsenschwanzsuppe (Oxtail soup)

8) Erdäpfelgulasch (Creamy potato goulash)

9) Griessnockerl-Suppe (Semolina dumpling soup)

10) Brotsuppe (Bread soup)

11) Bayerische Pilzsuppe (Cream of Mushroom Soup)

12) Kerbelsuppe (Cream of chervil soup)

13) Linsensuppe mit Saitenwurst (Lentil soup with Frankfurter Sausages)

14) Sauerkaut Tomates Suppe (Sauerkraut tomato soup)

15) Spargelsuppe (White asparagus soup)

1.3. Entrees

1) Rippchen mit Kraut (Kasseler Rippchen with Sauerkraut)

2) Rinderrouladen mit Kartoffeln und Rotkohl (German rouladen with potatoes and braised red cabbage)

3) Maultaschen (Swabian Raviolis)

4) Flammkuchen (Onion Cake with bacon)

5) Schweinshaxe in Bier Soße (Pork Knuckles in Beer Sauce)

6) Brathendl (Oktoberfest Roast Chicken)

7) Schweinebraten mit Kartoffelklößen (Pork Roast with Potato Dumplings)

8) Schweinegeschnetzeltes (Pork Stir Fry)

9) Zwiebelrostbraten (Pan Fried Beef Steaks With Fried Onions)

10) Sauerbraten (German style pot roast and gingersnap gravy)

11) Fleischküchle (Swabian meatballs)

12) Gefüllte Gans (Roasted Duck stuffed with apples)

13) Schwarzwald Cordon bleu (Black Forest Chicken Cordon Bleu)
14) Backhendl (Viennese fried chicken)
15) Wiener Schnitzel (Fried pork viennese)

1.4. Vegetarian

1) Linsen mit Spätzle   (Lentils with Spätzle)
2) Schupfnudeln (Finger-Thick Potato Dumplings)
3) Käsespätzle (Cheese pasta)
4) Schwäbischer Kartoffelsalat (Swabian Potato Salad)
5) Zwetschgenknödel (Plum Dumplings with Cinnamon Breadcrumb Butter)
6) Dampfnudeln mit Vanillesoße (German Steamed Dumplings with Vanilla Sauce)
7) Grünkernküchle (Green spelt burgers)
8) Kartoffelpuffer (Potato pancakes)
9) Semmelknödel mit Schwammerlsoße (Bavarian dumplings with mushroom sauce)
10) Pellkartoffeln mit Kräuterquark (Boiled potatoes with Quark)

1.5. Desserts

1) Zwetschgenkuchen (Plum cake)
2) Pfitzauf (Meringue Pastry)
3) Apfelstrudel (Apple Strudel)
4) Schwarzwälder Kirschcreme (Black Forest Cherry Cream Dessert)
5) Flambierte Crêpes im Waldbeerenmeer (Crêpes Flambees with Forest Berry Coulis)

6) Rote Grütze mit Vanillesoße (Red Berry Pudding with Vanilla Sauce)

7) Spaghetti Eis (Spaghetti Ice Cream)

8) Träubleskuchen (Swabian Redcurrant Tart)

9) Bienenstich (Bee sting cake)

10) Schneckennudeln (German Cinnamon Rolls)

11) Apfelküchle (Fried Apples)

12) Windbeutel (Bavarian Cream Puff)

13) Bayerische Creme (Bavarian Cream)

14) Ausgezogene (Knee pastries)

15) Buchteln (Sweet yeast buns)

2. Appetizers

1) Bibbeliskäs (Cottage Cheese With Onions And Herbs)

3 cups quark

1 cup heavy whipping cream

1 red bell pepper

1 yellow bell pepper

1 small bag of radishes

Dash of salt, pepper, and ground caraway seeds

1 cup Limburger cheese

Chives for garnishing

Mix the quark and heavy whipping cream in a bowl. Add salt, pepper, and ground caraway seeds to taste. Chop the bell peppers and radishes and sprinkle over the bowl. Dice the Limburger cheese and add it to the quark as well. Garnish with chives and serve.

2) Bayerische Brezen (Bavarian Pretzels)

1 package active dry yeast
1/8 cup warm water
1 1/3 cup warm water
1/8 tsp sea salt
4 ½ cups flour
2 tbsp baking soda

Preheat oven to 400°F.

In a bowl, dissolve yeast in 1/8-cup warm water. Stir in remaining warm water, salt, and flour. Knead dough until smooth and elastic. Dough does not need to rise.

In a saucepan, measure 2 tablespoons baking soda to each cup of water. Put enough water to fill the saucepan at least 3 inches high. Bring soda and water mixture to a light boil and simmer. Make sure the baking soda is well dissolved.

Cut the dough into eight pieces. Roll a long thick pencil shape with your hands but keep the middle a little thicker. Pick up both ends, cross to form rabbit ears and then twist the ends and pull them back to the rest of the loop.

Place aside on lightly floured surface and let rise about 10 minutes.

Place pretzels one at a time into the liquid baking soda mixture for 10-15 seconds. Using a large slotted plastic spatula, push each pretzel into the water to ensure it is fully covered.

Remove the pretzel from the liquid mixture and place onto a baking pan, lined with parchment paper.

Use a sharp knife and slit the thickest part of the pretzel lengthwise. Salt the top of pretzels with course ground sea salt as desired. Place the pan with the pretzels into the oven for 18-19 minutes or until pretzels are to desired darkness.

Tip: Pair with Bavarian sweet mustard, Weisswurst and smooth German Weissbeer to enjoy an authentic Bavarian meal.

3) Gebackener Camembert (Baked Camembert With Red Currant Sauce)

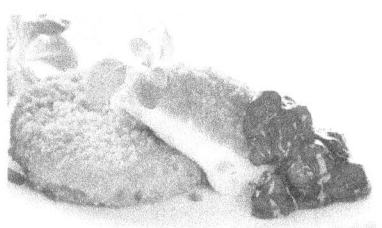

Four 4.5-ounce rounds Camembert cheese

2 cups flour

2 large eggs

1/2 cup whole milk

2 cups plain breadcrumbs

2 tablespoons extra virgin olive oil

2 tablespoons unsalted butter

8 ounces German red currant preserves

Parsley for garnish

Preheat oven to 450 degrees F.

Place the flour in a shallow dish. In a second shallow dish, whip the eggs and milk to create an egg wash. Place the bread crumbs in a third shallow dish.

Dredge the first round of Camembert in the flour and make certain it's completely coated. Remove the Camembert and tap off all excess flour. Place the floured round into the egg wash. Completely cover it with egg. Remove the Camembert from the egg wash, gently shaking it to remove any excess, and place it in the bowl containing the breadcrumbs. Completely cover the round in breadcrumbs and then remove it from the dish, tapping the cheese to remove all excess breadcrumbs. Repeat the process with the round so that it is double-breaded, and then repeat the entire process with the remaining rounds of Camembert.

Place the breaded rounds in the refrigerator while you prepare the pan for sautéing. It is important that you move quickly, as you do not want the breadcrumbs to get soggy.

Melt the olive oil and butter in a medium sauté pan over high heat. Remove the first Camembert round from the refrigerator and place it in the hot sauté pan. Sauté it on each side until light golden brown, about 1 minute each side. Repeat the process with the remaining rounds.

Place the rounds into your preheated oven and cook until the Camembert softens, 5 to 7 minutes.

Meanwhile, place the preserves in a medium sauté pan and warm over high heat.

Place a round on each serving plate. Spoon the warmed preserves onto the plate next to the baked Camembert. Garnish the top of each with parsley and serve immediately.

4) Obatzter (Bavarian Cheese Spread)

OBATZTER IS A TRADITIONAL BAVARIAN DISH CONSISTING OF CAMEMBERT CHEESE, BUTTER, PAPRIKA AND ONIONS. IT IS USED AS A SPREAD ON BREAD OR PRETZELS.

1 LB GERMAN CAMEMBERT CHEESE
8 OUNCES DOUBLE CREAM CHEESE (DOPPLERAHM-FRISCHKÄSE)
1 1/4 OUNCES BUTTER
6 TO 8 SPOONFULS DARK GERMAN BEER
1 LARGE ONION
SALT AND PEPPER TO TASTE
PAPRIKA

Mash together the Camembert cheese and the double cream cheese until well mixed. Blend the butter in to the mixture along with the salt, pepper and paprika. Pour over the beer and mix in to the mixture. (You can also use wine instead of beer). Serve with sliced onions, some hearty German bread or fresh pretzels.

5) Markklößchensuppe (Marrow Dumplings In Double Consomme)

Make the Consomme

1 lb ground beef

6 egg whites

1 cup carrots 1/4 inch dice

1 Cup celery 1/4 inch dice

1 Cup onions 1/4 inch dice

6 garlic cloves diced

1/2 cup of parsley stems chopped coarse

3 Bay leaves

10 peppercorns

2 quarts cold chicken or beef stock

Chop the vegetables and arrange the vegetables and spices on a plate.

 Put the ground beef in a bowl and add the egg whites. Reserve the egg yolks for the Markkloeschen.

Mix all the ingredients together in the bowl well.

Add the meat mix to the cold broth in a 4 qt soup pot (size of a Dutch oven)

Bring the stock now to a simmer, stirring gently so ingredients don't stick to the bottom.

Once the broth comes to a simmer, don't stir it anymore.

You want to let this mix congele like a meatloaf on top of the broth.

This is called a "raft". Let it simmer for 30 to 40 minutes.

There will be just a gentle bubbling in one corner of the little hole on the side of the raft.

After 30 -40 minutes turn off the stock and gently lift the raft off of the top of the consomme.

Put the raft in a pan and reserve. This can be used to make a nice meat sauce for spaghetti or Lasagna.

Strain the rest of the broth through cheesecloth or a loose towel

Make the Markkloeschen

1/4 cup marrow extracted from bones (instructions below)

1 egg (beaten)

1/3 cup breadcrumbs

1 teaspoon flour

a dab of baking powder (approximately 1/16 teaspoon)

dash nutmeg dash pepper

1 tablespoon parsley (chopped)

1/4 teaspoon salt

Wash the bones. Without removing the peel, wash the onion. Using a knife make a cut large enough to insert the bay leaf in the onion.

Press the cloves in the opposite end of the onion.

Combine all the soup ingredients in a large pot and cover with cold water (about 5 cups).

Bring to a boil, turn down the heat and simmer for three hours. Strain the stock through a fine sieve or through several layers of cheese cloth.

Place the stock in the refrigerator to cool quickly. When cool remove fat from the top. Heat to a boil and simmer until marrow balls are done. Season with salt and pepper to taste.

Take the bones and remove marrow with a knife or spoon. (You should have about 1/4 cup marrow.)

Strain the marrow through a fine sieve and beat until creamy.

Add the beaten egg, breadcrumbs, flour, baking powder, salt parsley, nutmeg, pepper and mix well. Let it sit for 30 minutes. Form little balls (marble size)

6) Badischer Wurstsalat (Bologna Salad From Baden)

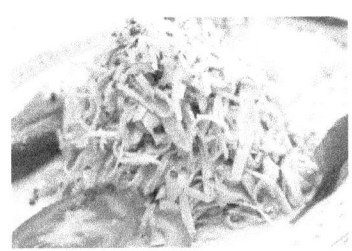

10-12 oz. bologna cut into thin strips

1 cup carrots cut into thin strips

1 cup diced tomatoes

1/3 cup diced onion

2 dill pickles (diced)

1 large Granny Smith apple cut in 1" pieces

3 hard boiled eggs

15 large green grapes sliced in halves

3 tablespoons sour cream

2-3 teaspoons cream style horseradish

1 teaspoon mustard

1/3 cup whipping cream salt, pepper

Place the bologna, carrots, tomatoes, onion, pickles and apple in a large bowl.

Dice the egg whites and add to the bowl.

Place the egg yolks in a small bowl and mash with a fork.

Stir in sour cream, horseradish, mustard and whipping cream.

Pour over the salad and stir.

Add the grapes, stir and season with salt and pepper to taste.

Serve with bread.

7) Bayerischer Krautsalat (Bavarian Cabbage Salad)

1 small head cabbage
Salt
1/4 lb. bacon
1 medium onion
4 tablespoons vinegar
1/4 teaspoon sugar
Salt and black pepper to taste
1 tablespoon cumin seeds, lightly crushed

Wash the cabbage. Slice into very thin strips. Place into a saucepan. Cover with cold salted water. Bring to a boil. Reduce heat and simmer 5 minutes.

Cut bacon crosswise into thin strips. Fry until crisp. Peel and chop the onion. Add to the bacon, sauteeing for 1 minute.

In a bowl, combine the cabbage, bacon and onion. In a separate bowl, blend the vinegar, sugar, salt, black pepper and cumin seeds. Pour over the cabbage, mixing well.

Cover and chill for at least 30 minutes to blend the flavors. Serve cold.

8) Käsedip (Quick Cheesedip)

3/4 tablespoon unsalted butter
1 tablespoon all-purpose flour
1/2 cup milk plus up to 2 tablespoons additional
3/4 cup grated cheese (I used sharp, orange-colored, cheddar)
1/8 to 1/4 teaspoon fine salt and cayenne pepper, or to taste
Melt the butter in a small saucepan over medium heat. Add the flour and cook for 1 minute, stirring all the time with a spatula. Whisk in half of the milk (about 1/4 cup) and cook until slightly thickened. Then gradually add the rest of the milk (1/4 cup) and cook until you get a creamy sauce – about 1-3 minutes.
Turn heat to low and stir in the cheese until smooth and all of the cheese is melted. You may add up to two tablespoons more milk if the consistency is rather thick.
Season with salt and cayenne pepper, to taste.

Enjoy immediately with Pretzel Bites, Taco Chips or anything else.

9) Sauerkaut-Schinken Bällchen (Kraut Ham Balls)

1 pound ground fully cooked ham
1 jar (16 ounces) sauerkraut, drained and chopped
1/4 cup finely chopped onion
2 tablespoons plus 3/4 cup dry bread crumbs, divided
1 package (3 ounces) cream cheese, softened
2 tablespoons minced fresh parsley
1 tablespoon prepared mustard
1/4 teaspoon garlic powder
1/8 teaspoon pepper
1/4 to 1/2 cup all-purpose flour
2 eggs
1/4 cup milk
Oil for deep-fat frying

In a large bowl, combine the ham, sauerkraut, onion and 2 tablespoons bread crumbs.

In another bowl, combine the cream cheese, parsley, mustard, garlic powder and pepper; stir into sauerkraut mixture. Chill for 1 hour or overnight.

Shape into 3/4-in. balls; coat with flour. In a small bowl, beat eggs and milk. Dip ham balls into the egg mixture, then roll in the remaining bread crumbs.

In a deep-fat fryer or electric skillet, heat oil to 375°. Fry ham balls until golden brown; drain on paper towels.

10) Rindfleisch Zwiebel Strudel (Beef Onion Strudel)

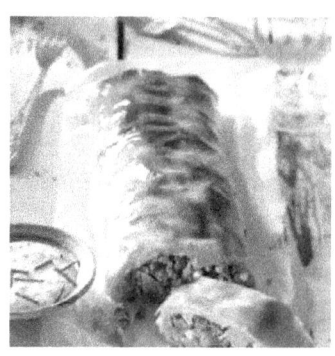

1-1/2 cups sliced sweet onions

1/4 cup butter, cubed

1/2 pound ground beef

1 teaspoon all-purpose flour

1 teaspoon brown sugar

1/2 teaspoon ground cumin

1/4 teaspoon salt

1/4 teaspoon pepper

1/2 cup beef broth

1 tube (8 ounces) refrigerated crescent rolls

3/4 cup shredded mozzarella cheese

2 tablespoons grated Parmesan cheese

In a large skillet, sautee onions in butter until browned and caramelized; remove with a slotted spoon and keep warm.

In the same skillet, cook beef over medium heat until no longer pink; drain.

Stir in the flour, brown sugar, cumin, salt and pepper until blended. Gradually add the broth; cook for 8 minutes or until liquid is absorbed. Stir in reserved onion.

Unroll dough and separate into four rectangles. Separate each rectangle at perforation into two triangles (see Fig. 1). Pinch two 6-in. sides together to form a triangle Repeat with remaining dough.

Place point of one triangle near the end of a greased baking sheet. Place point of second triable in center of first triangle. Repeat with remaining triangle .

Spoon beef mixture in a 1-1/2-in.-wide strip down the center; sprinkle with mozzarella cheese.

Starting at one end, fold alternating points across filling. Pinch ends to seal.

Sprinkle with Parmesan cheese.

Bake at 375° for 15-20 minutes or until golden brown.

Cool for 5-10 minutes before slicing.

11) Strammer Max (Hearty German Sandwich With Egg)

4 tbsp. unsalted butter

2 1/2" -thick slices country bread

4 slices prosciutto

2 eggs

1 tbsp. finely chopped chives

Kosher salt and freshly ground black pepper, to taste

Heat 4 tbsp. butter in a 10" skillet over medium-high heat.

Add bread slices and cook, turning once, until golden brown, 5-6 minutes.

Transfer bread to a plate and top each with 2 slices prosciutto.

Heat remaining butter in skillet and add eggs; cook until whites are cooked through and yolks are still runny, 2-3 minutes.

Top each sandwich with 1 egg, and sprinkle with ½ tbsp. chives and salt and pepper. Serve hot.

12) Speckbrötchen (Smoked Ham Rolls)

1 tbsp. active dry yeast

2 tsp. vegetable oil

7 1/2 cups flour

2 tbsp. plus 1/2 tsp. salt

2 tbsp. plus 1/2 tsp. sugar

10 oz. black forest ham, cut into small cubes

Dissolve yeast in 2 1/3 cups warm water in a small bowl; set aside until foamy, about 10 minutes. Grease a large bowl with oil and set aside.

Combine flour, salt, and sugar in another large bowl, add yeast mixture, and stir until dough is stiff. Turn dough out onto a floured surface and knead until smooth, about 15 minutes.

Knead ham into dough, shape dough into a ball, and transfer to prepared bowl. Cover bowl with a clean damp dish towel and set aside, in a warm spot, to let rise until doubled in bulk, 1–1 1/2 hours.

Lightly dust 2 sheet pans with flour and set aside. Turn dough out onto a clean surface, divide into 24 equal pieces, and shape each into a ball.

Put 12 dough balls on each pan, about 1" apart, cover with clean damp dish towels, and set aside, in a warm spot, to let rise until doubled in bulk, 1–1 1/2 hours.

Move one of the oven racks to center of oven and another oven rack to lower third of oven. Put a small pan of water on lower rack.

Preheat oven to 400°. Bake rolls until golden brown and hollow sounding when tapped, 25-30 minutes.

Transfer rolls to a cooling rack to cool.

13) Flammkuchen (Onion Flatbread With Bacon)

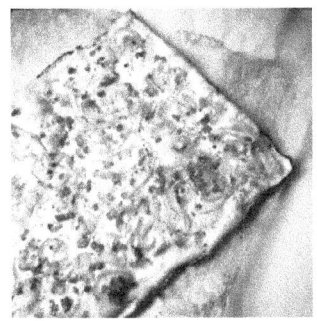

3/4 cup milk

5 tablespoons unsalted butter, room temperature, plus more for bowl

1/4 cup sugar

Salt

Grated zest of 1/2 lemon

3 large egg yolks

1 package active dry yeast

3 cups plus 1 1/2 teaspoons all-purpose flour, plus more for rolling out dough and wrap

3 strips bacon, cut into 1/2-inch dice

3 large onions, finely chopped

1/3 cup plus 2 tablespoons sour cream

1 large egg

1 teaspoon caraway seeds

Place milk and 4 tablespoons butter in a small saucepan, and heat until butter has melted. Remove pan from heat, and let mixture cool until tepid.

Place milk mixture in the bowl of an electric mixer fitted with the paddle attachment. On low speed, add the sugar, 1/2 teaspoon salt, lemon zest, egg yolks, and yeast. Gradually add 3 cups flour, creating a dough that is soft but not sticky.

Turn dough out onto a floured surface, and knead until it is smooth and elastic and springs back when you poke it with your finger, about 5 minutes. Place in a large buttered bowl, and cover tightly with plastic wrap.

Set in a warm place until dough has doubled in bulk, about 1 hour.

Heat oven to 400 degrees. Line an 11-by-17-inch baking sheet with parchment. Punch dough down, and roll out to a 1/4-inch thickness.

Place on prepared baking sheet, and cover with buttered plastic wrap; let rise until dough doesn't spring back when you poke it with your finger, about 20 minutes.

Melt remaining tablespoon butter in a large skillet over medium heat. Add the bacon, and cook until golden and crisp and most of fat has been rendered, about 6 minutes.

Add onions, and cook, stirring occasionally, until translucent, 8 minutes.

Reduce heat to low. Sprinkle 1 1/2 teaspoons flour over onions, and stir in.

In a small bowl, whisk together sour cream and the egg, and stir into the onion mixture. Cook, stirring, until mixture thickens, about 1 minute.

Remove skillet from heat, and season with salt.

Spread mixture on top of dough, and let rise 15 minutes more. Sprinkle top with caraway seeds. Bake until edges are crisp and brown, about 30 minutes. Transfer to a wire rack to cool, and serve.

14) Heringssalat (Herring Salad)

1 matjes herring per person (soused herring, a raw herring in mild brine)
tart apple
pickled beets
cornichons
shallot
roast pork, sliced (or chicken/turkey breast)
lingonberry preserve
crème fraîche
salt & pepper
Dijon mustard
bay leaf, allspice, pimento

Put crème fraîche and lingonberry preserve into large mixing bowl.

Chop the apple, beet, cornichons, shallot, herring and cold cuts and add to the bowl.

Add djion mustard, salt & fresh ground pepper to taste and mix well.

Add bay leaf, allspice and pimento, cover the bowl and let marinate in the refrigerator overnight -

or better yet for a day or two

15) Gefüllte Tomaten Mit Shrimps (Shrimp Stuffed Tomatoes)

Per person

3.5 oz cooked shrimp

1-2 tomatoes depending on size

Juice of ½ lemon

1 T parsley

salt and pepper

Tabasco sauce, optional.

2 T plain yogurt

Chop shrimp or place in food processor. Combine shrimp with parsley, lemon juice, yogurt, salt and pepper. Cover and refrigerate 30 min – 1 hour. Cut of top of tomato and scoop out inside. Fill with shrimp mixture and top with Tabasco if desired.

3. Soups

1) Gaisburger Marsch   (Beef & Vegetable Stew With Spätzle)

1 lb Beef
Water or Beef Broth (enough liquid so that beef and vegetables are completely covered as they simmer)
1/2 Onion, cut into large pieces
1 stick Celery
2 or 3 Carrots
1 lb Potatoes, raw & peeled 1 small bowl fresh Spätzle or dried Spätzle (available at most German Delicatessens)
Salt, Nutmeg
Onions, separated into rings
Butter
Fresh parsley, chopped

Prepare fresh Spätzle (or cook dried Spätzle according to package instructions).

In a large pot, combine beef, water (or broth), onions, whole stick of celery, and whole carrots. Bring to a boil. Reduce to a simmer and allow soup to cook until beef is soft - about 2 hours.

Cut raw potatoes into cubes. One half hour before beef becomes really soft, add potatoes to soup.

Remove beef from soup. Cut into cubes. Likewise, remove celery and carrots. Cut into cubes. Return beef and vegetables to soup. Add seasonings to taste.

In a frying pan, melt some butter. Fry onion rings until they are gold brown.

Divide soup into 4 soup bowls. Garnish with crispy onion rings and chopped parsley. Serve immediately

2) Leberknödelsuppe   (Liver Dumpling Soup)

1/2 lb Calf's or Beef Liver, finely ground
1/2 lb Ground Veal or Beef
3 day-old Bread Rolls
1 cups Milk
1 small Onion, finely chopped
1 tablespoon Butter
3 teaspoons Chopped Parsley
1 Egg
Bread Crumbs
Flour
Salt and Pepper
Marjoram
Beef Broth

Cut the bread into small cubes. Add to a bowl and pour milk over the bread. Allow to soak for 30 minutes. Squeeze out excess milk and set bread aside.

In a frying pan, melt butter. Cook onions in the butter until transparent.

Add onions to the bread cubes, along with the parsley and egg. Add ground liver and ground veal or beef. Add salt, pepper, and marjoram. Gently knead the mixture with your hands. Add bread crumbs and flour, just enough until a firm dough forms and that the dough holds together when forming dumplings.

Form ball-shaped dumplings.

In a large cooking pot, bring broth to a boil. Drop dumplings into the boiling broth, then reduce heat to a simmer. The dumplings are fully cooked when they float to the top of the broth.

To serve, pour some broth into 4 soup bowls. Add two dumplings to each bowl. Sprinkle some freshly chopped parsley over the dumplings for decoration. Serve immediately.

3) Zwiebelsuppe Mit Dunklem Bier (Dark Beer Onion Soup)

4 Brandt Zwieback toasts

4 onions

4 tbsp butter

32 fl oz beef broth

salt and pepper to taste

1 cup of dark beer (German Dark Oktoberfest Bier)

3 tbsp chopped chives

Preparation:

Peel onions and cut into rings. Heat half the butter and sauté onions until soft and translucent. Add broth and season with salt and pepper. Simmer for 10 minutes.

Soak the Zwieback briefly in the dark beer. Heat the remaining butter in a frying pan and fry the Zwieback on both sides till golden brown.

Serve the soup in bowls, topped with the browned Zwieback toasts and chopped chives.

(As an alternative to beer, sprinkle the Zwieback with celery and onion salt, top with cheese and grill in the oven before adding to soup.)

4) Bier Käse Suppe (Cheese Soup With German Lager)

1/2 cup unsalted butter
4 ounces Black Forest ham, diced
1 medium yellow onion, chopped
3 shallots, chopped
1 clove garlic, chopped
1/2 tablespoon chili powder
1/4 cup all-purpose flour
3/4 cup German lager
7 cups chicken stock
Pinch of cumin seed
2 cups shredded Allgäuer Emmentaler cheese
2 cups shredded Tilsiter cheese
Sea salt
Freshly ground white pepper
4 slices whole grain German bread, chopped
2 tablespoons chopped cilantro
Preparation:
In a stockpot, melt 1/4 cup of the butter over medium-high heat. Add the Black Forest ham, and sauté until golden brown. Add

the onion, shallots, garlic, and chili powder. Sauté until glossy, about 2 minutes.

Add the flour to create a roux. Whisk in the German lager and stock.

Add the cumin seed, and lower the heat to medium. Cook until the liquid is reduced by one-half, about 35 minutes.

Remove from heat and stir in the cheeses. Season to taste with salt and pepper.

To make the croûtons, melt the remaining butter in a medium sauté pan over high heat. Add the diced German whole grain bread, and pan-toast until crispy.

Pour into serving bowls and top with the croûtons and the cilantro. Serve immediately.

5) Flädlesuppe (Broth With Strips Of Pancake)

1 egg
¼ cup flour
3/8 cups milk
Dash of salt and pepper
2 tbsp. mixed herbs
1 onion
2 tbsp. sesame seeds
3 tbsp. canola oil
4 ¼ cups vegetable broth

Combine eggs, flour, milk, salt, pepper, and herbs into a bowl, forming a thin dough. Heat up 2 tbsp canola oil in a skillet. Make 3 thin pancakes from the dough, sprinkling them with sesame seeds while they are frying. Cut the pancakes into strips

Peel and chop the onion. In another pan, heat up the remaining canola oil and fry the onion, stirring occasionally until they are golden brown.

Bring the vegetable broth to a boil, adding the onions. Remove the soup from the heat and add the pancake strips. Let the soup sit for a few minutes before serving.

6) Pichelsteiner Topf (Pichelsteiner Stew)

1/2 pound boneless lamb shoulder

1/2 pound boneless beef chuck

1/2 pound boneless pork (from belly)

4 teaspoon butter or lard

32 fl oz. vegetable broth

3 large carrots

1.5 cups green or savoy cabbage

1 cup celeriac

1 cup leeks

1 cup celery

1 cup parsnips

1 cup kohlrabi or turnip

1/2 cup chopped onions

black pepper, salt

3-4 tbs parsley

3 medium sized, cut potatoes

1/2 cup Crème fraîche

1/4 lbs. bone marrow

– Peel and cut the vegetable into finger thick slices

– Cut all meat into 1-inch thick cubes.

– In a big skillet fry meat until it gets brown on all sides; scrape brown parts from pan; set aside
– Fry onions until brown an set aside
– Sautee vegetables and set aside

Now put all ingredients in a big pot, in layers one by one, sprinkling all layers with salt and pepper
– First the meat
– then onions
– then the vegetables
– then the potatoes

Pour over the vegetable broth, bring it to a boil over high heat, then reduce the heat to its lowest level and cover the pot tightly.
– Let is simmer for 1.5 hours and don't stir.
– Serve directly out of the pot.

7) Ochsenschwanzsuppe (Oxtail Soup)

1/2-2 lbs. oxtails

3 slices bacon (diced)

2 tablespoons oil

1 leek (washed and sliced)

1 medium onion (sliced)

2 carrots (sliced)

1/2 bunch parsley (washed and chopped coarsely)

2 whole cloves

2 medium bay leaves

1 tablespoon salt

12 cups cold water

4 tablespoons butter or margarine

1/2 cup flour

1 tablespoon lemon juice

1/3 cup red wine salt and pepper

Begin preparing this recipe either early in the morning on the day before.

Wash and thoroughly dry the oxtails. In a large kettle sauté the bacon for 1 minute.

Add the oil and brown the oxtails on all sides.

Add leeks, carrots, and onions and then sauté 5 minutes making sure they don't burn. (The soup will be a nice dark color if the oxtails are brown all over, but not burned.)

Add the water, salt, cloves, bay leaves and parsley.

Bring to a boil, turn down the heat and simmer for 2.5 to 3 hours. Strain the soup through a fine sieve, remove the tails and discard the remaining ingredients.

Place the soup in the refrigerator for 5 hours or overnight.

Once the tails cool cut off the meat and keep it.

After the soup has set in the refrigerator for the prescribed time, remove it and discard all the fat that has hardened on top of the soup.

In a large kettle melt butter or margarine and then add the flour. Sauté stirring continuously so it doesn't burn. When the mixture is light brown add the cold soup and stir until it boils.

If lumps occur strain the soup for their removal.

Lumps should not occur provided you add the soup when it is cold and stir constantly.

Add lemon juice, red wine, the meat and season with salt and pepper.

 Adding the meat is optional. Serves 6.

8) Erdäpfelgulasch (Creamy Potato Goulash)

4 big or 7 medium starchy potatoes (russets or yellow)

3 medium yellow onions

1 clove garlic

2 large smoked sausages

2 tablespoons Hungarian paprika

1 teaspoon Paprika

2 teaspoons vinegar (any kind will do)

1 tablespoon tomato paste

1 teaspoon marjoram

1 ¾ teaspoon caraway seeds, ground medium-fine with mortar and pestle

¾ teaspoon coriander seeds, ground medium-fine with mortar and pestle or ¼ teaspoon

½ teaspoon sugar

½ teaspoon fine salt

½ teaspoon freshly ground pepper

2 bay leaves

1 bouillon cube (for 2 cups broth)

7-8 cups water

Peel, wash and cut the potatoes into ¾ inch cubes.

Cut the onions in half lengthwise, and then finely slice them (half-rings).

Heat 2 tablespoons oil in a large pot, preferably non-stick.

Add the onions and cook over high heat for 5 minutes. Stir constantly. After 5 minutes reduce heat to medium and cook onions, stirring often, for about 15 minutes, or until soft and golden to light-brown in color.

Don't brown them too much as they will taste bitter.

Add garlic for the last 2 minutes (directly grate/press it into the pot).

Prepare a pot with 8 cups of hot water, you will gradually add more later.

When the onions are golden, add both types of paprika. There should be enough oil in the pot, so the paprika won't burn (= bitter taste).

Stir for 10 seconds and deglaze with vinegar.

Immediately add tomato paste, marjoram, caraway and coriander. Stir for a few seconds, then gradually add 1 cup of water while stirring.

Allow the liquid to reduce, then add another cup of hot water. Boil it down to a creamy consistency.

Add sugar, salt, pepper, bay leaves 1 crumbled bouillon cube.

With a ladle add about 1 cup of the hot water to the goulash (depending on your pot and heat, you will need the last cup). Stir each time after adding water.

Add the potato cubes and cook for ½ hour, without lid.

Meanwhile slice sausages (about ¼ inch thick) and add. Cook another 30 minutes, until the potatoes are just done.

. The sauce should thicken with this trick. If you let it cool (f.e. overnight) and heat the goulash again, its consistency will be thicker.

Serve with dark bread, bread rolls or some slices of baguette.

9) Griessnockerl-Suppe (Semolina Dumpling Soup)

5 ½ tablespoons unsalted butter, softened
2 eggs, lightly beaten (at room temperature)
2/3 cups white semolina (wheat farina, cream of wheat)
1/4 teaspoon fine salt
1/8 teaspoon ground nutmeg
1 tablespoon chopped flat parsley
Beef or vegetable stock (about 4 cups)
Chopped chives to garnishBeat softened butter with an electric hand mixer until creamy, about 1 minute.

Gradually add half of the beaten eggs, then half of the semolina. Add the remaining eggs, semolina, nutmeg, salt and parsley and mix until well combined. The mixture should be soft and creamy. Put the batter into the fridge and let it rest for 15
minutes, so it gets firm.

Bring a wide pot of generously salted water to a boil. Reduce temperature to medium-low. The water should simmer gently but not be boiling or the dumplings will fall apart.

Dip two tablespoons (to avoid sticking) into hot water and form tight, oval quenelles with the aid of 2 tablespoons, so they end up with three clear edges and a smooth surface.

If this is too difficult, you can wet your hands and shape them. The important thing is that they need to be really tightly shaped. Don't make them too big, as they will double in bulk.

Drop the formed dumplings into the simmering water. If you are using a rather small pot, don't overcrowd it, because the dumplings will plump up.

Cook the dumplings in barely simmering water for 5 minutes. Reduce temperature to the lowest possible and let them steep for another 10-15 minutes. By now, they should have doubled in volume. Try one dumpling, if it is still quiet firm in the center, let them steep for a couple more minutes. The dumplings should be soft but not mushy.

Meanwhile heat the stock. When the dumplings are done, transfer them with a slotted spoon into soup bowl. Add a ladle of stock and serve sprinkled with chopped chive.

10) Brotsuppe (Bread Soup)

2 lbs. stew meat
6 marrow bones or 2 lbs veal or beef stock bones
2 garlic cloves
1 leek, washed and sliced
2 celery stalks, chopped
2 small carrots, peeled and chopped
salt and pepper
1 1/2 quarts water
4 medium onions
3 tablespoons butter
1 unsliced loaf of Bauernbrot (peasant bread) or light rye bread
2 Tbsp. finely chopped fresh parsley
4-6 Tbsp. cream

Place stew meat, bones, garlic, leek, celery, carrots, and seasonings
in a large pot with the water; bring to a boil. Allow to simmer gently for at least 1 hour, skimming off the impurities from the surface.

Halve the onions and cut into semicircular slices. Sautee the onions in butter over medium-high heat, until they turn brown (stirring constantly to keep them from turning black). Add half of the onions to the soup; drain the other half on a paper towel and set aside.

Cut several slices from a loaf of peasant bread or light rye bread, as thin as you possibly can, and toast these golden brown in the oven. Break into pieces.

Strain the bones, stew meat, and vegetables from the broth. Distribute the toast pieces and the remaining crispy onions among the soup plates before pouring the broth over them. Garnish with parsley and float a little dab of cream in the middle of each plate of soup.

11) Bayerische Pilzsuppe (Cream Of Mushroom Soup)

3 tablespoons unsalted butter
1 medium yellow onion, finely chopped
1 pound cremini or button mushrooms, or ideally wild mushrooms, cleaned and sliced
2 tablespoons finely chopped flat-leaf parsley
Salt and freshly milled black pepper
3 cups vegetable broth or water, more to taste
1 cup sour cream
½ cup (2 ounces) flour
White vinegar
6 to 8 medium potatoes, boiled in their skins and peeled while still warm

Heat the butter over low to medium heat in a large saucepan and sauté the onions until translucent, do not brown. Add the parsley cook for 1 more minute.

Add the mushrooms and increase the heat to medium. Cook until they start to release liquid, stirring often. Season with 1 teaspoon salt and a bit of pepper. Add the broth, bring to a boil and cover. Simmer for 20 minutes.

In a small bowl, whisk the sour cream with the flour until well blended. Gradually add it to the cooked soup, whisking vigorously after each addition until it is fully dissolved before adding more.

This is to prevent lumps.

Bring the soup to a quick boil and continue whisking. It will be quite thick. Add more broth if you prefer a thinner soup.

Season with a dash of white vinegar, salt and pepper.

Serve hot with a boiled potato in each bowl.

12) Kerbelsuppe (Cream Of Chervil Soup)

6 oz. fresh chervil, stems and leaves separated
3 1/2 cups chicken stock
1/2 cup heavy cream
2 egg yolks
Kosher salt and freshly ground black pepper, to taste

Bring chervil stems and stock to a simmer in a 4-qt. saucepan over medium-high heat; simmer, covered, until stems are tender, 8–10 minutes.

Strain stock, discarding stems; return to pan and keep warm. Puree chervil leaves, cream, parsley, yolks, salt, and pepper in a food processor until smooth; transfer to a bowl.

Whisk 1 cup broth into yolk mixture, then slowly whisk into remaining broth until smooth.

13) Linsensuppe mit Saitenwurst (Lentil soup with Frankfurter Sausages)

1 ham hock or approx. 1 cup of dice ham
2 quarts Chicken, beef or ham stock (8 cups)
2 cups chopped onion (1 medium onion)
2 cups chopped celery heart, with green tops (stalks)
2 cups chopped carrots (3 large)
1 pound bag dry lentils sorted and cleaned
salt and pepper to taste
1 tablespoon dried savory leaves (May substitute dried thyme)
2 bay leaves
2 Tablespoons Hungarian paprika
a dash of nutmeg
6 Frankfurters with natural casing
You can use a Dutch oven or Crockpot for this.
Simmer the ham hock or ham with the bay leaves , herbs and spices for 2 hours to develop good flavor.
 Add the lentils and vegetables and simmer for 2-3 hours.
You can use thicken the soup, by taking 2 cups of the soup and puree them, or use a hand held Immersion blender and puree some of the soup right in he pot.

To serve ladle soup bowl 3/4 full put a heated Frankfurter on top and ladle another cup on top.

14) Sauerkaut Tomaten Suppe (Sauerkraut Tomato Soup)

2 pounds sauerkraut, rinsed and drained
1 can (28 ounce) diced peeled tomatoes
5 cups water
1 can (6 ounce) tomato paste
2 bay leaves
1/4 teaspoon freshly ground pepper OR more to taste
1/4 teaspoon seasoned salt OR more to taste
1 1/2 pound lean beef sirloin OR beef top round steak, trimmed of fat and
cut into 1/2-inch cubes
2 1/2 tablespoons sugar
3 tablespoons fresh lemon juice

In a 5- OR 6-quart electric slow cooker, combine sauerkraut, tomatoes with
their liquid, water, tomato paste, bay leaves, pepper, seasoned salt and
beef.

Cover and cook on high heat setting 3 hours. Reduce heat to low setting and
continue cooking, covered, 3 1/2 hours longer, or until beef is tender.
Remove and discard bay leaves. Stir in sugar, lemon juice and more seasoned
salt and pepper to taste, if needed. Serve immediately.

15) Spargelsuppe (White Asparagus Soup)

1 lb. white asparagus, woody ends removed
4 cups low-sodium vegetable broth
1 small yellow onion, chopped
1 6 oz. container creme fraiche
1/2 medium lemon, juiced
 kosher salt, to taste
ground black pepper, to taste
1 tsp. olive oil
1 tbsp. fresh chives, chopped (for garnish)

Trim white asparagus by cutting off bottom inch of stalks. Dice the asparagus into 2 inch pieces. Dice onions to similar size.

Heat olive oil in large dutch oven or soup pot over medium high heat. Sautee onions until softened, but not browned, about 8 minutes. Add asparagus slices and sautee for 5 minutes, or until coated with olive oil and beginning to turn translucent.

Add broth to cover asparagus and onions. Bring to a boil. Lower heat to medium low and simmer, uncovered, for 30-40 minutes or until asparagus is tender. The asparagus should be able to be easily pierced by a fork.

Using an immersion blender, blend the soup until a smooth texture develops. Add creme fraiche and blend until incorporated.

Serve topped with chives or green asparagus tips.

4. Entrees

1) Rippchen Mit Kraut (Kasseler Rippchen With Sauerkraut)

4 - 6 Kasseler Rippchen
2 lbs Potatoes
Salt
1 Onion, finely chopped
1 tablespoon Butter
2 lbs Sauerkraut (ready-made in a jar or can)
1 cup Dry White Wine
5 Juniper Berries (optional)
1 1/2 cups Milk
1 tablespoon Butter

Add one tablespoon butter to a large cooking pot. Add onions and cook until transparent.
Drain some of the Sauerkraut juice. Add the Sauerkraut to the cooking pot - loosen it with a fork if necessary. Add white wine

and optionally the juniper berries. Bring to a simmer and allow to cook for 30 minutes.

Add Kasseler Rippchen to the Sauerkraut and cook for 15 minutes.

Wash and peel potatoes. Cut into large pieces. Add to a large cooking pot. Add enough water so that potatoes are covered. Add a little salt. Bring to a boil and allow to cook until potatoes are soft. Mash the potatoes with a potato masher. Mix in milk and one tablespoon butter.

To serve, add Sauerkraut to each plate and place one Kasseler Rippchen on top of the Sauerkraut. Serve with the mashed potatoes.

2) Rinderrouladen Mit Kartoffeln Und Rotkohl (German Rouladen With Potatoes And Braised Red Cabbage)

8 slices beef, inside round, sliced thinly for Rouladen

1 onion, sliced thinly

8 dill pickle quarters

4 slices smoky bacon, cut in half

Toothpicks

Gravy:

2 tablespoons oil

1 or 2 slices bacon chopped

2 cups beef broth

2 tablespoons cornstarch

¼ cup cold water

½ cup heavy cream

Salt and pepper to taste

Preheat oven: 350°F.

Oven proof casserole or baking dish with lid – spray lightly with Pam.

Lay each slice of meat on a clean board. Lightly salt and pepper each side and pound with a meat mallet.

On one end, lay a half slice of bacon, a quarter spear of dill pickle, and several thin slices onion.

Tightly roll up each piece and secure with a toothpick.

Brown each roulade on all sides in hot oil in a large stainless steel or caste iron fry pan. Transfer to casserole dish. Keep warm in oven while preparing the beef broth gravy.

For Gravy: Sauté the chopped raw bacon and left over onion slices in the pan you used to brown the meat until bacon is limp and onions are translucent. De-glaze the pan by pouring the beef broth onto the onions and bacon and stirring until all the brown bits have left the sides of the pan.

Pour the beef broth mixture on the rouladen in the casserole. Cover with a lid. Bake in preheated oven about 2 ½ hours.

When rouladen are fork tender, carefully remove from casserole and arrange on a meat platter. Cover with foil to keep warm.

Dissolve the cornstarch in the ¼ cup cold water. Pour beef broth into saucepan. Bring to a boil. Add cornstarch mixture and whisk until bubbly and thickened. Slowly pour in cream. Do not bring to a boil. Just heat the gravy through. Season gravy with salt and pepper to taste.

Serve with boiled potatoes

Braised Red Cabbage (Rotkohl):

2 tablespoons vegetable oil

1 medium onion chopped

6 apples, cored and diced, unpeeled

1 head red cabbage, shredded

Cider vinegar

Sugar, salt and pepper to taste

In a large dutch oven, sauté onions and apples in oil until softened.

Add shredded purple cabbage.

Add 2 tablespoons cider or white vinegar. Stir vegetables. Add 1 cup water.

Cook on medium heat, stirring occasionally until mixture comes to a boil. Turn heat down to low and simmer for 1 to 1 ½ hours or until cabbage is tender.

Taste for seasoning. Add more vinegar, sugar and salt (pepper optional) to taste.

Heat through before serving.

Left over red cabbage can be frozen in freezer bags or containers for up to 3 months.

3) Maultaschen (Swabian Raviolis)

3 eggs

pinch of salt

for each egg, half an eggshell of water

1.5 cups wheat flour

Mix eggs with salt and water. Sift flour into a bowl and make a well in the middle. Break the eggs into it and blend all the ingredients together. Take out of the bowl and then knead the dough on a board until air pockets can be seen when the dough is cut. You can knead by hand or with a mixer.

Depending on the flour, if the dough is too thick add a little water or an egg white. The dough shouldn't be too soft. Form a ball and place on a board. Cover with a cloth and leave to rest.

Now you can prepare the filling

1.5 cups fresh spinach

saltwater

1 oz diced bacon

1 oz butter

1 small onion, finely chopped

3-4 stale rolls, crusts removed

5 oz ham or cold meat, diced

10 oz ground meat (pork or beef)

2-3 eggs

a pinch of salt, pepper and nutmeg

boiling saltwater or meat broth

Clean the spinach well, wash and blanch it briefly in boiling saltwater. Rinse with cold water, let it drain and chop coarsely. Braise the bacon in butter for a couple of minutes, add the chopped onion and spinach and braise for a couple more minutes. Soak the stale rolls in water until soft. Squeeze out the excess water and chop the rolls into pieces.

In a large bowl mix the above prepared ingredients with ham and ground meat. Add the eggs and season with salt, pepper and nutmeg.

On a floured surface roll out the noodle dough into rectangular sheets (about twice as wide as you want your Maultaschen to be). Use a tablespoon of filling at equally spaced 3 inch intervals all down the middle of one side of the sheet of dough. Fold the plain half of the sheet of dough over to cover the filling and press firmly on the spaces around the pockets of filling. Use a pastry wheel or cookie cutter to cut into 3 inch squares.

Put them into boiling saltwater or meat broth and let simmer (not boil) for 10-15 minutes depending on the size.

They can be served in broth with toasted bread crumbs and parsley or with onion rings.

Alternatively, slice an onion and fry the rings in butter until brown and serve with the soup.

If there are any left over, they can be used the following day. Cut into one inch slices, fry in fat, add slightly beaten eggs and milk to the pan and cook through. Delicious served with a crisp green salad.

4) Zwiebelkuchen (Onion Cake With Bacon)

1 package Pillsbury™ Refrigerated Pie Crust

2 tablespoons butter

2 1/4 pounds yellow onions, finely diced

5 slices thick cut bacon, finely chopped

1 1/2 cups full fat sour cream

4 large eggs

2 tablespoons Gold Medal™ unbleached all-purpose flour

2 teaspoons salt

1 teaspoon caraway seeds plus more for sprinkling

Gather up the ingredients. Grease a 9-inch springform. Preheat the oven to 400°F.

In a Dutch oven or heavy skillet over medium-high heat fry the bacon until crispy.

Add the onions and butter and cook them for about 25-30 minutes until light golden brown. Remove from heat and let the mixture cool.

Combine all remaining filling ingredients in a medium bowl and stir well to combine.

On a lightly floured surface, gently roll out one of the refrigerated pie crusts just enough to extend it by an inch or so in diameter. Lay the pie crust into the springform, lightly pressing it do the bottom and sides, leaving about an inch border from the top of the pan.

Add the onion mixture to the filling mixture and stir until combined.

Pour the filling into the springform and sprinkle a few caraway seeds on top.

Bake for 50-55 minutes or until the Zwiebelkuchen is golden brown on top and the filling is firm when pressed in the center. Best served warm. Also excellent reheated the next day.

5) Schweinshaxe In Bier Soße (Pork Knuckles In Beer Sauce)

4 extra small pork knuckles, about 24 oz

Coarsely ground pepper

Coarsely ground salt

2 tbsp vegetable oil

1 1/4 cup beef broth

1 cup dark beer (Oktoberfest beer)

2 onions

17 1/2 oz celery root (celeriac)

3-4 tsp cornstarch to taste

Wash pork knuckles and dry with kitchen towel.

Mix salt and pepper and rub pork knuckle all around

Heat oil in pan and brown pork knuckles all around at medium heat.

Add beef broth and bake in preheated oven at 400 F° on medium level for 1 hour 40 minutes.

Mix beer with 1 tsp. salt and pour every 15 minutes over the knuckles.

Cut onions in quarters, wash celery root and cut into 1/3 in slices.

Add vegetables to the pork knuckles at around 1 hour and ten minutes and mix with meat juices. Increase heat to 425 F° approx.. 30 min before end of cooking.

Take knuckles and vegetables out of the pan, cover and keep warm. Season sauce with any spices or simply with salt and add cornstarch to taste and favorite thickness.

Serve knuckles with vegetables, spätzle, knoedel or mashed potatoes, sauerkraut or red cabbage.

6) Brathendl (Oktoberfest Roast Chicken)

1 whole chicken, about 3.5 pounds

1 tsp salt

1 tsp paprika (sweet)

¼ tsp dried thyme

¼ tsp oregano

1 pinch ground pepper

¼ tsp marjoram

1 pinch of ground rosemary

2 tbsp butter

Wash the whole chicken inside and out, and thoroughly towel dry.

Mix the herbs and spices in a bowl. Rub the chicken inside and out with the spice mixture.

Place the chicken in a baking dish filled with 1/2 in of water. Cut the butter into small pats, and place on top of the chicken. Roast at 325 degrees for about one hour, or until done. Baste with the pan juices several times during the roasting, every 15-20 minutes.

Serve with Pommes Frites (French fries) and radish and a German pretzel or with potato dumplings and red cabbage.

7) Schweinebraten mit Kartoffelklößen (Pork Roast with Potato Dumplings)

4 lb boneless pork loin joint

3 teaspoons German mustard

1 teaspoon basil

1 teaspoon sage

1 teaspoon marjoram

2 tablespoons butter

4 strips bacon

1 carrot

1 bunch parsley

1 onion

1/2 cup red wine

Rub the meat with the mustard, sprinkle with herbs and salt and lay in a roasting dish. Fry the bacon in the butter and pour over meat.

Roast in a preheated oven at 400 degrees F for approximately 90 minutes until juices run clear and meat is no longer pink (use a meat thermometer to check correct internal temperature is reached). Periodically pour water over roast (about 3/4 cup).

In the meantime, chop the carrot, parsley and onion. Add wine and vegetables to roast after 40 minutes.

Serve with German potato dumplings (Kartoffelklößen) and German red cabbage (Rotkohl).

8) Schweinegeschnetzeltes (Pork Stir Fry)

9-ounce box German spätzle or fresh made
1-pound pork loin
tablespoons unsalted butter
2 cups mushrooms, sliced
1/2 cup yellow onion, diced
3/4 cup white wine
2 to 3 tablespoons cream (to taste)
salt and pepper to taste

Prepare spätzle according to box instructions or make fresh and let drain thoroughly. Slice pork into strips and season with salt and pepper. Heat 1 tablespoon butter in a skillet and cook pork over medium heat until cooked through and slightly browned. Remove pork from pan.

Using the same pan, heat the remainder of the butter and cook mushrooms and onions over medium heat until soft and slightly browned.

Deglaze the pan with white wine and simmer until reduced by half. Add cream to taste.

Place the pork and peas back into the pan and heat just until warmed through. Serve with prepared spätzle.

9) Zwiebelrostbraten (Pan Fried Beef Steaks With Fried Onions)

4 slices rib steak (7 oz. ea.) may use sirloin as well.

salt and fresh ground pepper

4 med. onions

lard for frying in skillet

one glass of red wine

4 Tbsp. sweet cream

Score edges of steaks so they don't curl

season with Salt and pepper

Fry steaks in a heavy cast iron skillet to desired doneness

Cut onions in thin rings and fry crisp in hot lard in pan

Arrange on top of meat.

Boil the meat juices together with the glass of red wine, allow to thicken

(reduce) and stir in the sweet cream Serve this sauce with the steaks

Good with Spätzle and a Salad

10) Sauerbraten (German Style Pot Roast And Gingersnap Gravy)

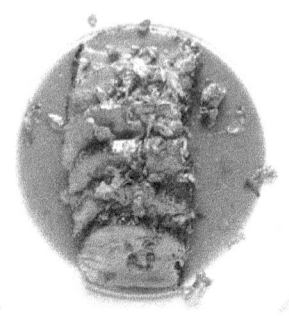

1 (5-lb.) beef eye of round
2 cups red wine
1 1/2 cups red wine vinegar
3 large onions, thinly sliced
1 large carrot, thinly sliced
1 bouquet garni (1 tbsp. pickling spices,
14 whole cloves,
8 whole black peppercorns,
3 bay leaves,
3 sprigs thyme,
2 sprigs parsley, wrapped in cheesecloth, tied with kitchen twine)
4 tbsp. unsalted butter
4 slices bacon, finely chopped
3 tbsp. flour
2 tbsp. sugar
1/2 cup golden raisins

6 gingersnaps, crumbled

Juice of 1/2 lemon

2 tbsp. chopped parsley

Kosher salt, to taste

Season beef liberally with salt in large bowl. Bring wine, vinegar, 1 onion, carrot, bouquet garni, and 4 cups water to a boil in a 4-qt. saucepan; pour over beef.

Cover and refrigerate, turning once or twice a day, for 5 days. Remove beef from marinade; pour marinade through a fine strainer into a bowl, and dry beef thoroughly. (Reserve 5 cups of the marinade and the bouquet garni.) Heat 2 tbsp. butter and bacon in an 8-qt. Dutch oven over medium-high heat; cook until bacon renders its fat, about 10 minutes.

Transfer bacon to a plate; set aside. Add beef; cook, turning, until browned all over, about 25 minutes. Transfer to a plate; set aside.

Heat oven to 325°. Add remaining onions to pot; cook, stirring, until caramelized, about 18 minutes. Return beef to pot with reserved marinade and sachet; boil. Cover; bake until beef is very tender, about 2 1/2 hours. Transfer beef to a platter; pour sauce through a fine strainer into a bowl.

Return pot to medium-high heat; add remaining butter.

Add flour and sugar; cook, whisking constantly, until lightly browned, about 5 minutes.

Add sauce, raisins, gingersnaps, and juice; return beef to sauce. Bring to a simmer, cover pot, and cook until slightly reduced, about 10 minutes.

Thinly slice beef; arrange on a platter.

Spoon sauce over top; sprinkle with bacon and parsley.

11) Fleischküchle (Swabian Meatballs)

1 (12oz.) can evaporated milk
6 C. flour
4 eggs, beaten
1 tsp. salt
1 lb. ground pork
2 lbs. ground beef
1 tsp. garlic salt
1 small onion, chopped

In a large bowl, mix the milk with the flour. Once the milk is absorbed, add the eggs. Mix into a firm dough, adding more flour if necessary. Let the dough rise while you mix together the pork, beef, garlic salt and onion. Heat oil in a deep fryer to 375 degrees.

 Divide dough into balls the size of an egg. Roll each ball of dough into a circle. Scoop and flatten meat mixture on one half of the circle. Fold over dough and seal the edges. Deep fry until golden brown (about 5 minutes). Be sure to turn while frying. Drain on paper towels.

Serve with potato salad

12) Gefüllte Gans (Roasted Duck Stuffed With Apples)

1 young duckling

salt, pepper, paprika

1 onion

2.1 oz butter

1.5 cups water

some beer for basting

1 teaspoon potato or corn starch

5-6 medium sized tart apples (i.e. Granny Smith)

Thaw the duckling over night in the fridge. Next day remove the giblets pack from the inside of the duck. Rinse duck with cold water inside and out. Pat dry with paper towels. Cut off the neck skin and the tail section, where most of the fat is stored. Make a cut in the skin on the breast side towards the tail. Remove any fat from under the skin if necessary. Season duck inside and outside with salt, pepper and a little paprika.

Wash and peel the apples, remove core. Cut in wedges and fill the duck as necessary, do not overfill because the duck could fall apart during roasting. Close opening by sawing together. Place duck in a roasting pan, breast down, tie the legs together and tuck under the wings (or tie them as well). This prevents the duck loosing shape during roasting and to much browning of the legs and wings.

Add the into wedges cut onion to the bottom of the roasting pan with a little of hot water, melt the butter and pour evenly over the duck. Roast uncovered in a pre-heated oven (390°-420° F on medium or lower rack) for 1.5 - 2 hours. When the back of the duck is browned turn duck breast side up. Baste duck several times during roasting and in the last 10 minutes baste the duck with the beer or salty water and increase the temperature to 450° F. This will create a nice crusty skin.

Remove duck from roasting pan, remove ties and apples and let duck rest covered with tin foil. Remove the onions from the pan, loosen drippings, remove fat from sauce (optional) by transferring it into a Gravy Separatoror if you make the duck a day ahead, you can finish the gravy the next day. Transfer the gravy strained into a small pot and place in the fridge over night. The next day you can scrape off the hardened fat from top with a spoon.

Finish the sauce: Heat the gravy if needed and season to taste. Thicken if necessary with the starch. Add 1 teaspoon of starch into a small cup filled half with cold water, stir to create a thin paste. Add to the simmering sauce, stir and simmer until thickened.

Heat the duck in the oven on low temperature until hot. Plate the duck, cut into portions, on a decorative plate and place the baked apples around the duck (which can be eaten as well).

Sides are Spätzle (German home-made noodles) or Knödel (German home-made dumplings) and Rotkohl (red cabbage).

13) Schwarzwald Cordon Bleu (Black Forest Chicken Cordon Bleu)

4 boneless skinless chicken breasts, butterflied
1/4 tsp paprika
1/2 tsp granulated garlic
1/4 tsp each sea salt and freshly ground whole black peppercorns
4 1-oz slices German Limburger cheese rind removed
8 slices German Black Forest ham
1 1/2 cups flour
4 eggs, beaten
1 1/2 cups bread crumbs

Fresh flat-leaf parsley (optional)
Preparation:
Preheat oven to 375 degrees F.
Season each butterflied chicken breast with paprika, garlic, salt, and pepper on all sides. Lie each piece flat on a cutting board; place 2 slices of ham and 1 slice of cheese inside each. Fold over to seal the chicken breast. Insert a wooden toothpick at each end to seal.

Dredge chicken breasts in flour, egg, and then bread crumbs. Place on a baking sheet lined with parchment paper. Dot with vegetable oil and bake until chicken reaches 180 degrees F, about 10 minutes. Garnish with chopped parsley, if desired.

14) Backhendl (Viennese Fried Chicken)

Chicken, cut into serving pieces -- 3 pounds

Lemon juice -- 2 tablespoons

Salt and pepper -- to season

Flour -- 1 cup

Eggs, beaten with a little water -- 2

Breadcrumbs -- 1 1/2 cups

Oil for deep frying

Toss the chicken in a large bowl with the lemon juice, salt and pepper. Set aside to marinate for at least 30 minutes.

Put the flour in one bowl, the eggs in another bowl and the breadcrumbs in a third bowl.

One at a time, dip the chicken pieces first in the flour, then in the egg, and finally in the breadcrumbs to coat.

Set the breaded chicken pieces on a baking sheet to let the coating set.

Heat the oil to 370°F.

Deep fry the chicken pieces for 10 minutes, or until lightly browned.

Reduce heat to low and continue to cook for another 20 minutes, turning often.
Drain on paper towels and serve hot.

15) Wiener Schnitzel (Fried Pork Viennese)

1 small pork tenderloin, less than 1 pound

salt, to taste

pepper, to taste

1 cup white panko bread crumbs

2 large eggs

2 cups + 1 tablespoon vegetable oil

lemon wedges, for serving

First, place the pork tenderloin on a clean surface. Cut it in half on a 45-degree angle. Place each piece of pork between plastic wrap, and pound with a meat pounder (or rolling pin) until roughly 1/4" thick. It should take on a rough half-moon shape if you place the pointed end down while pounding.

Sprinkle each pounded cutlet with salt and pepper, and set aside.

Next, heat 2 cups of the oil in a large Dutch oven until it reaches 375-degrees F.

Meanwhile, add the bread crumbs to a shallow dish.

Add the eggs plus 1 tablespoon of the oil in another shallow dish.

Dip the cutlets in the egg mixture, followed by the breadcrumbs. Use your hands to firmly press the crumbs into the meat. Let the cutlets sit and dry a bit while the oil finishes heating.

Once the oil is up to temperature, carefully arrange both cutlets in the pan. There should be ample room if you're using a standard Dutch oven pot.

Fry the cutlets for about 1-2 minutes on each side, until they are golden brown.

Serve with lemon wedges.

5. Vegetarian

1) Linsen Mit Spätzle   (Lentils With Spätzle)

This dish is considered the "National Food" of Swabian (Schwaben). It began as a food for the poor people of Swabian, who couldn't afford meat. Lentils were a good alternative because of their heartiness and nourishment, especially during the winter months.

Fresh Spätzle or 1 package dried Spätzle (available at most German Delicatessens)
2 cups dried Lentils
1 Onion, cut in half
8 cups vegetarian bouillon
2 Cloves
1 teaspoon Salt
2 teaspoons Tomato Paste
Salt, Pepper, Marjoram, Thyme (to taste)
In a large cooking pot, soak the lentils in water for 12 hours to soften them.

Press cloves into onion halves.

Drain lentils and add the vegetarian bouillon , onions halves, and 1 teaspoon salt. Bring to a boil. Reduce heat and allow mixture to simmer for 1 hour.

In the meantime, prepare fresh Spätzle or cook dried Spätzle according to package instructions.

Remove onion halves from the soup.

Mix tomato paste and seasonings into the soup.

Serve immediately and serve with the Spätzle.

2) Schupfnudeln (Finger-Thick Potato Dumplings)

1 lb potatoes

2 eggs

1 cup of flour + extra set aside for kneading

a few pinches of salt not too much

1 pinch nutmeg

Boil and peel potatoes. Press potatoes through a ricer. Kneed into a dough with remaining ingredients. Bring a salted pot of water to a rolling boil. Flour your surface well.

Roll dough into long finger thick strips, squeeze into palm so they have tips on both ends. Drop into boiling water for about 5 minutes until they float. Serve any way you like them.

Traditionally they are fried with bacon and sauerkraut. But you can also serve 1/2 a serving with a low fat stew to make it healthier. The recipe is calculated for 4 servings but could easily be 8.

3) Käsespätzle (Cheese Pasta)

3 cups all-purpose flour

4 eggs

2 teaspoons salt

1 cup water

2 tablespoons butter

8 ounces cheese, grated

fried onions

Combine flour, eggs, salt, water and mix to a firm, smooth dough using an electric mixer until it is smooth and detaches easily from the side of the bowl. Cover and allow to sit for about 30 minutes.

Bring a large pot of water to the boil and generously add salt. There are several methods to cook the spätzle. You can either pass the dough through a wide-holed sieve into boiling water, to which salt has been added, or you can spread it in batches onto a board and scrape it off into the boiling water. Alternatively you can also use a special spätzle press.

Regardless of the method, make sure to make the spätzle in small batches and once it rises to the top of the pan and floats on the surface, remove the spätzle with a slotted spoon rinse in cold water.

In a greased casserole dish layer the spätzle and cheese alternately and sprinkle each layer with a little pepper. Finish with a layer of cheese and sautéed or crispy onions. Bake in the oven at 450 degrees F for about 5 to 8 minutes.

4) Schwäbischer Kartoffelsalat (Swabian Potato Salad)

2.2 pounds small Yukon gold potatoes, all about the same size
1 small Vidalia onion, finely chopped
1 cup light vegetable broth (or chicken broth), hot
1/4 teaspoon sea salt, or more to taste
1 pinch white pepper
2 tablespoons white wine vinegar
3 tablespoons neutral flavored oil, such as canola or sunflower
the steamer basket in the bottom of the pot and add water until it touches the steamer. Bring to a boil. Add the potatoes, arranging them evenly on the steamer surface. Cover and cook until the potatoes are fork tender, about 20 to 30 minutes. Drain.

Allow to cool until you can hold the warm potatoes without getting burned. Peel and slice the warm potatoes.

While the potatoes cook, stir together the onions and the hot broth and set aside. When finished slicing the steamed potatoes, warm the broth mixture until hot.

Put the sliced potatoes in the large bowl. Pour on the broth mixture and sprinkle on the sea salt and pepper, then add the vinegar and oil. Carefully turn the potatoes to distribute the seasonings, but try to avoid breaking the slices. Typically served warm, but you can also serve chilled.

5) Zwetschgenknödel (Plum Dumplings With Cinnamon Breadcrumb Butter)

2-3 medium russet potatoes

1 egg, beaten

1/4-1 cups all-purpose flour

1 pinch salt

12 fresh prune plums, pitted (or 6 regular plums, or 12 high-quality dried prunes, soaked in warm water)

1 cup plain breadcrumbs

3 tablespoons unsalted butter

Granulated sugar

Ground cinnamon

Place 2-3 whole, unpeeled potatoes in a pot, cover with cold water, and put on the stove on high. Boil until the potatoes are tender when pierced with a fork. Drain and allow to cool until cool enough to handle.

Peel and gently mash the boiled potatoes.

Over-mashing will lead to heavy dumplings, so be gentle.

Add egg and a pinch of salt to the potatoes and mix just enough to combine.

Begin adding the flour, starting with 1/4 cup. You should add just enough flour to form a firm, malleable dough. The amount will depend on the size and water content of your potatoes and egg. Last time I used about 2/3 cup.

Form the dumplings. For each dumpling, take a piece of dough about the size of a golf ball. Roll it gently in your palms to form a rough ball. Then use your thumb to create a deep indentation in the center of the ball. Place a plum in the indentation and use your fingers to mold the dough around the plum. Be sure to completely envelope the plum in dough.

Bring a large pot of water to boil. Gently drop the dumplings into the water, making sure that they aren't too crowded. Boil, over high heat, until the dumplings all float to the top, about 15 minutes. Remove the dumplings with a slotted spoon.

Meanwhile, melt 3 tablespoons of butter in a saute pan over medium-low heat. Add the breadcrumbs and cook, stirring, until the breadcrumbs are golden and fragrant.

To serve, split the Zwetschgenknödel and top with plenty of breadcrumbs. Sprinkle with sugar and cinnamon to taste.

6) Dampfnudeln Mit Vanillesoße (German Steamed Dumplings With Vanilla Sauce)

Dumplings:

1 pound 2 ounces all purpose flour

1 cup warm milk (105-115 degrees F), divided

2 teaspoons active dry yeast

1 pinch sugar

1 large egg

1 1/2 teaspoon salt, divided

2 cups water

3 tablespoons unsalted butter

Vanilla Sauce:

2 egg yolks

4 1/4 cups milk, divided

1 1/2 ounces cornstarch

2 ounces sugar

1 vanilla bean

To make the vanilla sauce, add egg yolks to a small bowl. Beat with a hand mixer until thick and creamy.

In a small bowl, whisk together 6 tablespoons milk and cornstarch.

In a small saucepan, whisk together remaining milk and sugar. Scrape in the seeds from the vanilla bean and add the pod. Bring to a boil over medium heat, stirring constantly. Remove the vanilla pods and whisk in the cornstarch and milk. Continue to boil and stir for 2 minutes, until thickened. Remove from heat. Slowly pour a couple of tablespoons of the mixture into the beaten eggs while stirring. Pour the warmed eggs into the pot, stirring constantly, and return to medium heat. Bring to a boil for about 30 seconds before removing from heat again. Serve warm or refrigerate until chilled.

In a large bowl, add flour and make a well in the center. Pour in 1/4 cup of the warm milk and sprinkle with yeast and sugar. Gently stir the yeast into the milk and a small amount of the flour. Cover and let rest for 20 minutes, until the yeast becomes frothy.

Pour in the remaining milk, egg, and 1/2 teaspoon salt. Mix together with your hands and knead until smooth. Divide the dough into 8 equal pieces. Roll each piece into a ball and place on a lightly floured surface. Cover and let rest for 40 minutes.

In a wide pot or large, deep skillet, combine water and remaining salt. Bring to a boil and add the butter. Once melted, arrange the dough in the pot with 1-2 inches between each ball. Cover with a tight lid and reduce heat to low. Simmer for 20 minutes without removing the lid. Remove lid once all liquid has evaporated and dumplings have a crust on the bottom (there will be a crackling sound). Remove pot from heat and gently take out dumplings.

Serve with vanilla sauce and powdered sugar.

7) Grünkernküchle (Green Spelt Burgers)

4 oz Grünkern (green spelt groats)
1 garlic clove, minced
1 oz sunflower seeds
1 tbsp vegetable bullion powder
1 onion, finely chopped
½ bunch parsley, finely chopped
½ small beetroot, grated
1 tsp curry spices
1 tsp salt
1 tsbp spelt flour or 1 egg (optional)
6 oz hot water
2 EL coconut oil
To serve: green salad, sliced avocado or guacamole, sauerkraut
Directions:
Mix the spelt groats with the garlic clove, sunflower seeds, the vegetable bullion powder, the finely chopped onion, parsley, beetroot, curry spices and salt in a sauce pan. Add hot water up until that all ingredients are just about covered with a few still peaking out. Bring to a boil, then reduce heat and stir for about

3-4 minutes until you have a quite dry mass that is starting to come together in a big clump.

Take off heat and leave to stand for another 30 minutes for the spelt groats to soak up more water. Add egg or spelt flour if you feel the mass does not clump together very well yet.

Divide the dough into small burgers and fry for 5-10 minutes on each side over medium heat in coconut oil in a frying pan.

Serve with salad on the side, some guacamole and/or sauerkraut.

8) Kartoffelpuffer (Potato Pancakes)

3 large russet potatoes (about 2 1/2 lb.)

2 medium yellow onions

1/3 cup flour

3 eggs

Kosher salt, to taste

Ground white pepper, to taste

Canola oil, for frying

Applesauce, for serving

Peel potatoes and onions, and finely grate using a box grater. Place in a strainer set over a bowl and let drain, squeezing mixture until dry; transfer to another bowl.

Slowly pour off the water from squeezing the potatoes until you reach the milky starch at the bottom of the bowl; pour this on top of the drained potato mixture.

Add flour and eggs, and season with salt and white pepper; mix until evenly combined.

Heat 1/4 cup oil in an 8" skillet over medium heat.

Working in batches, measure out 1/2 cup potato mixture, and use your hands to flatten it into a 4-5" pancake; add to skillet, and fry, flipping once, until golden brown and cooked through, about 8 minutes.

Transfer to a paper towel-lined baking sheet, and repeat with more oil, as needed, and remaining potato mixture. Serve pancakes with applesauce on the side.

9) Semmelknödel Mit Schwammerlsoße (Bavarian Dumplings With Mushroom Sauce)

7 oz dry white bread or 6 day old rolls
6.8 fl oz lukewarm milk
salt
freshly ground black pepper
freshly ground nutmeg
1 onion
1/2 bunch flat-leaf parsley
1 T butter
2-3 eggs
flour or breadcrumbs

For the mushrooms :
1.3 lbs fresh mushrooms
1/2 lemon (about 3 T juice)
1 onion
1/2 bunch flat-leaf parsley
2 T butter
salt
freshly ground black pepper

6.8 fl oz cream

For the dumplings, cut the bread in small cubes or thin slices, put in a bowl, and douse with the lukewarm milk. Add salt, pepper and nutmeg, then let sit for 20 minutes.

Clean the mushrooms by rubbing shortly under water. Let them dry then cut them in thin slices. Sprinkle with 2 T lemon juice.

Peel both onions and wash and dry the whole bunch of parsley. Finely chop the onions and parsley.

For the dumplings, melt 1 T butter in a small pan, then cook half th

e onions until transparent. Mix in half of the parsley and cook shortly. Add the egg and the onion-parsley mixture to the bread mixture and combine everything well. Add salt, pepper and nutmeg to taste.

In a large pot, bring 2 liters of salted water to a boil. Make a small test dumpling and carefully place it in the boiling water for a short time. If it falls apart, add some flour or bread crumbs to the dumpling mixture. Then, with moistened hands, make 8 dumplings. Carefully put them in the boiling saltwater and allow them to cook over medium heat for 20 minutes.

For the mushrooms, melt 2 T butter in a large pan.

Add the rest of the chopped onion and cook until transparent. Add the mushrooms to the pan, stirring constantly. Add salt and pepper and the cream and let the mixture simmer for 10 minutes. Add the rest of the parsley and stir. Add salt, pepper and lemon juice to taste.

Take the finished dumplings from the water and allow to drip dry. Serve with the mushroom sauce.

10) Pellkartoffeln Mit Kräuterquark (Boiled Potatoes With Quark)

2 lb. small waxy potatoes, scrubbed
1 tsp. caraway seeds, plus ½ tsp. ground
16 oz. quark or Greek yogurt
3/4 cup minced chives
3 tbsp. milk
2 tsp. flaxseed oil
Kosher salt and freshly ground black pepper, to taste

Bring potatoes, caraway seeds, and 6 cups water to a boil in a 4-qt. saucepan; reduce heat to medium and cook until tender, 15–20 minutes. Drain potatoes, discarding caraway seeds; keep warm.

Stir ground caraway, quark, ½ cup chives, the milk, flaxseed oil, salt, and pepper in a bowl; garnish with remaining chives and serve alongside potatoes.

6. Desserts

1) Zwetschgenkuchen (Plum Cake)

7 ounces (200 g) all-purpose flour

pinch of salt

1 package dried fast-action yeast

1 1/2 oz (40 g) butter, at room temperature

5 tablespoons superfine sugar

1 small egg, beaten

3 1/2 fl oz milk, lukewarm

about 1 3/4 lbs plums, pitted and quartered

1 oz almond flakes

grated zest of 1 lemon

Mix the flour with the yeast, rub in the butter, then mix in 3 tablespoons of the sugar. Make a well in the center then beat in the egg and milk until you have a soft, smooth dough. Mix well in the bowl and knead for about 4 minutes.

Grease a 10 inch shallow, round, spring-form cake pan. Roll or pat out the dough to fit the pan. Dip your fingers in the flour if

the dough sticks. Press it in lightly, taking it right to the edge. Cover and leave to rise until doubled
in size, about 1/2 to 1 hour.
Arrange the plum quarters skin-side-down in circles on top. Sprinkle over the remaining sugar.
Heat the oven to 350 degrees F and bake the cake for about 35 to 40 minutes until it is risen and the plums are soft.
Cool in the pan and scatter over the almonds and lemon zest. Remove from the pan and cool completely on a wire rack.

2) Pfitzauf (Meringue Pastry)

1 cup flour
2 1/8 cups milk
4 eggs
1/8 cup sugar
1/3 melted butter
Dash of salt
1 tsp. cinnamon (optional)

Preheat oven to 300º F.

For the dough: mix the flour and milk together in a medium-sized bowl. In a small bowl, whisk together the eggs, sugar, salt, and cinnamon (if desired). Bit by bit add this mixture to the flour and milk mixture. Lastly mix in the melted butter.

Fill greased muffin pans with the dough. Initially bake for 25-30 minutes at 300ºF. Turn up the temperature to 350º and finish baking for another 15 minutes.

Serve with warm vanilla sauce and fruit compote.

3) Apfelstrudel (Apple Strudel)

Crumb mixture:
3 tablespoons unsalted butter, cut into tablespoons
1 cup fresh bread crumbs
1/3 cup sliced almonds
Apple filling:
1 1/2 pounds (about 4 apples) Granny Smith apples, peeled, halved, cored and very thinly sliced
1 teaspoon finely grated lemon zest
2 tablespoons lemon juice
1/3 cup golden raisins
1/2 cup granulated sugar
Assembly:
8 sheets phyllo dough (each sheet measuring 12" x 17")
6 tablespoons unsalted butter, melted
Confectioners' sugar for sprinkling
Make crumb mixture: In a large skillet, melt butter over medium heat. Add bread crumbs and cook over medium-high heat, stirring constantly, until crumbs are golden brown. Stir in the sliced almonds and set aside to cool.
Make filling: Place apples slices in large bowl and toss with lemon zest, lemon juice and raisins. Add sugar and toss to coat.

Assemble strudel: Position a rack in center of oven and preheat oven to 375 degrees F. Lay a sheet of phyllo on a clean work surface. Lightly brush sheet with butter.

Sprinkle with 2 1/2 tablespoons bread crumb mixture. Layer remaining 7 sheets phyllo over first, buttering and sprinkling each one with bread crumb mixture. Spoon apple compote evenly down long side of phyllo, about 2" from bottom edge and 1" in from both sides.

Fold bottom edge and side flaps over filling and roll up phyllo jelly roll-style.

Transfer strudel to baking sheet and brush it lightly with melted butter.

Bake for 30 to 35 minutes, or until crisp and golden. Remove strudel from oven and let cool on baking sheet on wire rack for 10 minutes.

Dust with confectioners' sugar and serve, sliced, with whipped cream.

4) Schwarzwälder Kirschcreme (Black Forest Cherry Cream Dessert)

1 vanilla bean

1 cup milk

3 egg yolks

1/4 cup sugar

4 envelopes/sheets unflavored white gelatine

2 shots (4-8 cl) of Kirsch (Kirschwasser)

2 tablespoons chocolate shavings

1 cup heavy cream

1/2 pound Morello cherries (preserved)

For the garnish:

2 oz. dark chocolate, lemon balm leaves, cherries

In a medium saucepan, add the vanilla bean to the milk and bring to a near boil. Take out the vanilla bean, cut it open and scrape the seeds into the milk. Mix the egg yolks with the sugar and add to the hot milk. Continuously whisk the mixture until it comes to a boil. Add the re-hydrated gelatin and the Kirsch and place in the refrigerator for about half an hour.

Whip the cream with an electric mixer. Fold the whipped cream and the chocolate shavings into the chilled mixture. Divide the cream evenly among 6 dessert glasses or one big glass bowl and place them back in the refrigerator. Purée the preserved Morello cherries and pour on top of the cream.

Garnish with cherries dipped into melted dark chocolate.

5) Flambierte Crêpes Im Waldbeerenmeer (Crêpes Flambees With Forest Berry Coulis)

4 tablespoons brandy

4 tablespoons orange liqueur

3 tablespoons forest berry jam

2 oranges

2 lemons

1 cup confectioner's sugar

3 tablespoons Crème de Cassis

2/3 lb. forest berries, fresh or frozen, plus more for decorating

1 tablespoon butter

1 tablespoon cognac

1 pinch of salt

1/2 tablespoon vanilla sugar

1/2 cup milk

1 egg

3 tablespoons confectioner's sugar

1/3 cup plus 3 tablespoons flour

Sift the flour and confectioner's sugar into a mixing bowl. In a separate bowl combine and beat the egg and the milk. Add the liquid ingredients to the flour mixture under constant stirring. Add the vanilla sugar, salt and cognac to the mixing bowl. Let the mixture rest for about 10 minutes.

Meanwhile, wash and clean the fresh forest berries or thaw the frozen fruit. In a medium saucepan combine the berries, Crème de Cassis and confectioner's sugar and boil for 3-4 minutes. Add the juice of 1 lemon. Let the sauce cool down and pour it onto four serving plates.

Melt the butter in a pan suited for crêpes-making and prepare four thin crêpes. If necessary place them in a 120-150° oven to keep them warm.

Combine the juice of 1 lemon and 2 oranges with the orange liqueur, add the forest berry jam and heat the mixture. Fold the crêpes twice (to form quarters) and place them into the sauce. Douse with brandy and carefully light the liquid. Arrange the crêpes on the serving plates, decorate with fresh berries, dust with confectioner's sugar and serve immediately.

6) Rote Grütze Mit Vanillesoße (Red Berry Pudding With Vanilla Sauce)

For the fruit pudding:
2 lbs. mixed berries (fresh or frozen) and
pitted cherries, washed and picked over
1/4 cup bottled fruit syrup or a good fruit juice
(raspberry, strawberry, or any other fruit you are using)
sugar
1/4 cup of cornstarch
For the vanilla sauce:
3 egg yolks
3 tablespoons sugar
1 tablespoon cornstarch
1 1/2 cups milk
1 vanilla bean, or
1 tablespoon pure vanilla bean paste
For the pudding:
Bring the blueberries and cherries to a boil in a large saucepan until they pop or release their juice. Hull the strawberries and cut very large ones into quarters. Add the more delicate fruit like

strawberries and raspberries last. Stir in the syrup and sugar to taste.

Dissolve the cornstarch in at least 1/4 cup cold water. Remove the pan from the heat, stir the cornstarch into the fruit mixture, and cook briefly over low to medium heat, stirring constantly. Make sure not to undercook the pudding, otherwise it will taste chalky. When the pudding turns clear and thickens, remove the pan from the heat immediately. Continue stirring for another 1 to 2 minutes.

Pour the hot pudding into a glass serving bowl or individual dessert bowls. To prevent the glass from cracking when you pour the hot pudding into it, put a damp dishtowel underneath the bowl. Refrigerate for several hours until set. Serve the pudding cold, but take it out of the refrigerator 30 minutes before serving, so it can develop its full flavor.

For the vanilla sauce:

Whisk the egg yolks with the sugar and cornstarch. Add the milk and vanilla. If using a vanilla bean, slit it lengthwise, scrape out the seeds with a sharp knife, and add the bean and the seeds to the mixture. Cook over low heat until the sauce thickens, whisking constantly. Mare sure that the sauce does not boil. Remove vanilla bean, if using. Refrigerate. Stir the sauce before serving.

7) Spaghetti Eis (Spaghetti Ice Cream)

1 quart vanilla ice
whipped cream
20 strawberries or raspberries
Strawberry or Raspberry jam or sauce
coconut, almond or white chocolate

Using a slotted spoon or large dipper (the one with small round holes), carefully press the well frozen vanilla ice cream through the holes onto a bed of whipped cream so that the strings of ice cream resemble spaghetti.

Top with strawberry or raspberry sauce and fruit and sprinkle with coconut, almonds, white chocolate or white marzipan sliver.

8) Träubleskuchen (Swabian Redcurrant Tart)

For the shortcrust pastry dough:

1 3/4 cups all purpose flour

1/2 cup fine sugar

3 tablespoons ground hazelnuts (if you don't like them or are allergic, exchange them for the same amount of flour)

a pinch of salt

1 stick unsalted butter, fridge cold, cut into small cubes

1 egg, cold

dried beans for blind-baking

For the filling:

4-5 tablespoons bread crumbs

1 1/2 pounds redcurrants

egg whites from 5 eggs

2/3 cup fine sugar

Combine the dough ingredients either in a kitchen machine or by hand. If using a kitchen machine, pulse the flour, ground hazelnuts (if used), sugar and salt until well mixed and then add the butter cubes until the ingredients are combined into coarse crumbs; add as much egg as it takes to just hold the dough together. If doing it by hand, mix the flour, sugar, salt and ground hazelnuts in a bowl and rub the butter cubes into the mixture until all butter is immersed and coarse crumbs form; also add as much egg as it takes to just hold the dough together.

Quickly form the dough into a ball and flatten it into a disc, wrap it in cling film or aluminium foil and refrigerate until dough is firm, at least 30 minutes.

Preheat oven to 360° F (conventional oven).

Roll out dough on a lightly floured surface or - if you have the same difficulties that I have with that task – between two sheets of clingfilm or baking parchment. Always only roll away from and towards you, then turn dough by 90° and repeat. Repeat until it reaches a dimension that covers the bottom of the springform pan plus minimum 2.5 inches on the edges of the form. Remove all excess flour from the dough with a brush. Carefully lift the dough and place it into the springform pan, press dough against the bottom and edges. Cut rough edges with a pizza slider or a pastry cutter.

Pierce the dough with a fork all over to allow steam to escape.

Let the dough chill in the fridge for another 10 minutes. Then, closely cover the dough with baking parchment, fill in dried beans up to the edge of the dough and blind-bake it at 360°F (conventional oven) for 15 minutes. Let cool for 10 minutes.

Meanwhile, beat the egg whites with an electric mixer until they form stiff peaks. Add the sugar and beat for further 4-5 minutes. Lastly, add the corn starch and mix in for another minute. Set aside 1/4 of the egg white to use on top of the tart. Carefully fold in the red currants under the remaining 3/4 of the egg white.

Sprinkle the breadcrumbs over the dough. Spread the redcurrant/egg white mixture over the dough with a spatula or spoon, top with the remaining egg white.

Bake at 360° F(conventional oven) for about 45-50 minutes. After approximately half the time, cover the pie with aluminium foil or baking parchment to prevent the meringue on top getting too dark. Cool on a rack.

9) Bienenstich (Bee Sting Cake)

DOUGH

4 and 1/2 cups flour

1 oz (1 tbsp) or 1 package dry yeast

1 tsp sugar

1 2/3 cup milk

1 / 2 cup sugar

1/2 tsp salt

1 small egg

1 /4 lb (1 stick) of butter softened

1 teaspoon lemon rind

Topping

1/3 lb (1 and 1 / 3 stick) Butter or margarine

1 cup sugar

1 tablespoon vanilla extract or vanilla Sugar

2 tablespoons milk

1 1/2 cups almonds sliced

2 tablespoons lemon juice

FILLING

1 4.75 oz. pk vanilla pudding

2 cups milk

1 / 4 lb (1 stick) Butter

Put flour into bowl, make a well in the middle, pour in the room temperature milk
1 teaspoon of sugar and the yeast. Let this sit for a few minutes to let the yeast activate, then
mix together.
 Add the remaining sugar, salt, egg and lemon rind. Cut the butter into slices and mix into the dough. Knead until smooth.
 Roll out the dough and fit it onto a greased cookie sheet. Let rise for 20 minutes or until doubled.
Prepare the Topping and Bake the Cake
preheat the oven to 375 degrees
Bring milk and butter to a simmer and add the sugar and nuts and cook till
smooth and the milk is absorbed. Stir in the lemon juice.
 Spread the topping on the dough and bake the cake for 35 minutes.
Prepare filling while the cake is baking.
Heat the milk on the stove to a simmer.
Add the vanilla pudding and cook for 1 minute, remove from stove and let cool
slightly.
Cut butter into small chunks and blend into the pudding one at a time.
Cut each cake in half and spoon about 2 -3 tablespoons filling onto bottom half, and replace top.
Smooth the filling on the sides of the cake.
Lay slices on a platter and serve with coffee or tea

10) Schneckennudeln (German Cinnamon Rolls)

Dough

3 1/3 cups flour

3 tbsp. sugar

1/2 tsp. salt

1/4 fast rise yeast or tbsp. fresh yeast

1/3 cup unsalted butter

1/2 cup milk, plus

2 tbsp. milk

2 large eggs

Combine flour, sugar, salt and yeast in large mixing bowl. Melt butter in the milk over very low heat and beat in eggs. Stir milk/butter into the dry ingredients to make the dough. Knead for 10 minutes. When itis springy and smooth, form a ball and put in a greased bowl. Cover with a dish towel and leave in a warm place for 1 hour or until doubled in size.

FILLING:

1/4 cup melted butter

1/3 cup sugar

1/3 to 1/2 cup Nestle Nesquik chocolate powder

2 to 3 tbsp. cinnamon

To shape, roll dough to 15 x 10 rectangle. Spread 1/4 cup melted butter evenly over dough. Sprinkle with mixture of sugar, Nesquik and cinnamon. (Add more Nesquik and/or cinnamon if you desire). Start with 10 inch side, roll up tightly, pressing edges to seal. Cut into 12 slices, (approximately 1 inch-thick pieces) place cut side down in greased 13 x 9 inch greased baking pan. Cover loosely with plastic wrap and cloth towel. Let rise in warm place 30 minutes (if you made the dough from scratch, you do not need to do this step.)

To bake, heat oven to 350*F. Uncover and bake for 20 to 30 minutes or until light golden brown.

GLAZE:

1 cup powdered sugar

1 to 2 tbsp. milk

1/2 tsp. vanilla

Combine all ingredients. Blend until smooth. Spoon over warm rolls.

11) Apfelküchle (Fried Apples)

4.4 lbs or about 10 Apples

6 Eggs

4 Cups Flower

2 Tbsp Sugar

2 Tbsp Baking Soda

4 Cups Milk (approximately)

1.5-2 Lbs Lard (or some sort of fat to fry in)

sugar

cinnamon

For the Dough: Mix eggs, flour ,sugar, salt and backing soda then add enough milk while mixing it with a hand mixer to make it a creamy fluffy liquid

Apples: peel them and remove the seeds cut them in 0,5cm thick ring

 How-To: Heat lard up very hot dip the slices into the dough(one at a time) and put them into the hot lard for as long as it takes to get that brownish delicious look take them out and put them directly into a mix of sugar and cinnamon

12) Windbeutel (Bavarian Cream Puff)

Puffs:

1/2 cup butter (unsalted if you can get it)

1/4 cup water

1/2 cup flour

Dash salt (only if using unsalted butter)

2 large eggs

Filling:

1 cup heavy whipping cream

4 oz. softened cream cheese

1/4 cup powdered sugar

1/2 tsp. almond extract

powdered sugar for sprinkling on top

Heat oven to 400° (375° if convection).

In a saucepan, heat the butter and water to a rolling boil.

Stir in flour (and salt, if using) all at once and beat vigorously about 1 minute, or until a ball forms.

Remove from heat and beat in eggs, 1 at a time, until batter is smooth and glossy.

Drop by 1/4 cupfuls onto an ungreased baking sheet about 3 in. apart.

Bake 35-40 minutes (less if convection) until puffy and golden brown all over.

Cool completely on wire rack.

For Filling:

Beat whipping cream, cream cheese, sugar and extract in a deep bowl until fluffy and holds its form well. Keep chilled until use.

Just before serving, split the puffs, remove any damp insides and fill with the cream mixture. Looks nicest if you use a fluted pastry tube for this.

Place caps back on puffs and sprinkle with powdered sugar; serve immediately.

13) Bayerische Creme (Bavarian Cream)

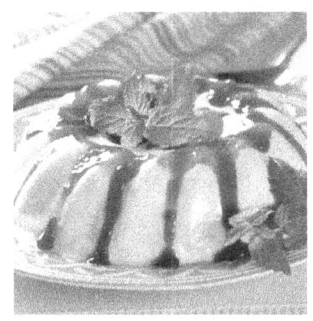

1 pkg. (8 oz.) cream cheese, softened
1/4 cup granulated sugar
1/2 teaspoon grated lemon peel
1 pkg. (3 oz.) lemon gelatin
1 cup boiling water
1/2 cup cold water
2/3 cup (5 fl.-oz. can) Evaporated Milk
1 tablespoon lemon juice
1 cup (12-oz. jar) raspberry jelly

Beat cream cheese, sugar and lemon peel in large mixer bowl until smooth. Dissolve gelatin in boiling water in medium bowl; add cold water. Gradually add gelatin mixture to cream cheese mixture; beat until smooth. Refrigerate mixture to a consistency of unbeaten egg whites.

Pour evaporated milk into small mixer bowl; place beaters into evaporated milk. Freeze for about 15 to 20 minutes or until ice crystals form around edges of bowl.

Beat on high speed until soft peaks form.

Add lemon juice; continue beating an additional 2 minutes or until mixture is stiff.

Immediately fold into gelatin mixture.

Spoon into 6-cup mold.

Refrigerate for at least 2 hours or until firm.

TO SERVE: Dip knife in warm water and run knife around rim; gently shake to loosen. Invert onto serving dish. Stir jelly until smooth. Pour 1/4 cup over top of mold. Serve with remaining jelly.

14) Ausgezogene (Knee Pastries)

1 1/4 sticks Unsalted Butter

4 Eggs

2 cups Milk

1/2 cup Sugar

Pinch of Salt

1 package Yeast

Enough Flour to make a firm dough

Oil for frying

Powdered Sugar

In a small bowl, combine the yeast and 1/2 cup of the milk (lukewarm). Mix in 3 tablespoons flour and 1 teaspoon of the sugar. Allow this mixture to sit in a warm place for 1 hour.

Combine remaining dough ingredients then add in the yeast mixture. Mix until a smooth dough forms, then knead by hand. Allow dough to sit in a warm place until double in volume.

Knead the dough to eliminate the pockets of air. Divide dough into tablespoon size pieces. Press flat each piece of dough. Allow dough pieces to rise again for 1 hour.

Heat oil in a large pot or deep fryer.

Take each piece of dough and stretch it out again - large enough that it would be able to cover your knee. Fry each stretched-out piece of dough until golden brown on both sides. Remove from oil and allow to drip dry on paper towels. Dust with powdered sugar.

15) Buchteln (Sweet Yeast Buns)

½ cup plus 2 tablespoons warm milk

1 ½ teaspoons active dry yeast

3 tablespoons sugar

1 large egg

5 ½ tablespoons melted butter

½ teaspoon vanilla extract

¼ teaspoon salt

2 ½ cups all-purpose flour

About 5 tablespoons apricot jam with fine texture (no chunks)

3 tablespoons melted butter for the pan

Confectioners sugar for dusting

In a large mixing bowl sprinkle the yeast over the warm milk and set it aside for 10 minutes for the yeast to dissolve and activate.
Stir in sugar, egg, melted (lightly cooled) butter, vanilla and salt with a hand whisk.
Stir in about 1 ½ cups of the flour to get a thick batter and stir vigorously with the whisk until no lumps remain. Time to change

your tools: Get rid of the whisk an use a sturdy (wooden) cooking spoon to gradually stir in the rest of the flour.

When all ingredients come together fold the edges into the center for a couple of minutes. Keep your dough in the mixing bowl for that. The dough will be sticky, but refrain from adding more flour. It helps if you oil your clean hands before you knead a sticky dough. Knead until smooth, about 5 minutes.

Let the dough rise, covered at warm room temperature until doubled in volume (about 3/4 to 1 hour).

Transfer the dough onto a lightly floured surface and divide it into 12 equal parts. Keep pieces you don't need right away covered.

Fold the edges of each piece into the middle a couple of times so you will get a nice ball with a smooth surface on the bottom side. Flatten each ball with your palm to a circle with a diameter of 3 to 3 ½ inch, keeping the center slightly thicker than the edges. Usually this part works without using any additional flour. If the dough keeps sticking to your counter top, add some.

Put 1 teaspoon of apricot jam (not more) in the center of every circle. Wrap the dough around the filling, pinching and sealing it tightly. Round the buns again, creating a bit of surface tension. If you use too much filling, it's difficult to seal them. Also avoid getting jam onto your edges, because this way it is almost impossible to seal them (see more troubleshooting in the note).

Put every Buchtel with the sealed side down onto a lightly floured surface until you have finished filling all of them.

Put about 2 ½ tablespoons melted butter (you might need a little more) in a small bowl. Brush a baking pan (I used an oval 11 x 7 inch ceramic pan) with melted butter, just until coated. Put every Buchtel in the bowl with the melted butter, turn it around until well coated.

Place the Buchteln, coated with butter, in your baking pan.

You can do this tightly packed (traditional way) or give them a little, but not too much space. They will still rise during the second proofing and baking. If you feel there are too many of them, you can place the remaining in a lined muffin tin.

Let them proof a second time for about 20-30 minutes at warm room temperature until puffy. It is best to cover the whole pan with a lid or cling wrap in this step. If you have a rather shallow pan, don't cover the Buchteln, since they will stick to the plastic wrap. If you couldn't cover them and they seem kind of dry before baking, you can brush them another time with melted butter.

Bake them at 375 °F in the preheated oven (center) for about 25 minutes (minimum 20 minutes). When they are golden-brown in color, take them out of the oven.

Let the Buchteln cool for 5-10 minutes and serve them dusted with confectioner's sugar.

www.ingramcontent.com/pod-product-compliance
Lightning Source LLC
Chambersburg PA
CBHW071439070526
44578CB00001B/151